101 Great Classroom Games

101 Great Classroom Games

Easy Ways to Get Your Students Playing, Laughing, and Learning

Alexis Ludewig and Amy Swan, Ph.D.

McGraw-Hill

New York   Chicago   San Francisco   Lisbon   London   Madrid   Mexico City
Milan   New Delhi   San Juan   Seoul   Singapore   Sydney   Toronto

The McGraw·Hill Companies

Library of Congress Cataloging-in-Publication Data

Ludewig, Alexis.
    101 great classroom games / by Alexis Ludewig and Amy Swan.
       p.   cm.
    Includes index.
    ISBN 0-07-148124-9
    1. Educational games.   2. Education, Elementary—Activity programs.   I. Swan,
Amy.   II. Title.   III. Title: One hundred one great classroom games.   IV. Title: One hundred
and one great classroom games.

    LB1029.G3 L83   2007
    371.33′7—dc22   2006046944

1 2 3 4 5 6 7 8 9 10 11 12 13 14 15 16 17 18 19 20 21 22 23 24 QPD/QPD 0 9 8 7

ISBN-13: 978-0-07-148124-3
ISBN-10:   0-07-148124-9

Interior illustrations by Monica Baziuk
Interior design by Monica Baziuk

McGraw-Hill books are available at special quantity discounts to use as premiums and sales
promotions, or for use in corporate training programs. For more information, please write to the
Director of Special Sales, Professional Publishing, McGraw-Hill, Two Penn Plaza, New York, NY
10121-2298. Or contact your local bookstore.

This book is printed on acid-free paper.

Dedicated to Jerry. With his support and encouragement, all things are possible.

—A.A.L.

Dedicated to Ally, who always inspires me and invites me to play.

—A.E.S.

Contents

· ·

Acknowledgments

• •

THIS BOOK WOULD not have been possible without our editors, Holly McGuire and Charlie Fisher. We thank Holly for the original concept and her faith in us as authors and Charlie for guidance through this process. We owe our thanks to the teachers who have shared their game ideas and favorites with us, especially Holly Geiger, Diane Repp, and the staff at Parker Lower School.

We want to thank our mom, Lois Ludewig, who began the tradition of teaching in our family and played games with us at home before taking them into her classroom. Her encouragement throughout this project was unflagging. Thanks also go to our dad, Bill Ludewig, whose sense of humor has permeated our existence.

A special thank-you goes to Ally Nisenoff, a creative soul, who seems to invent a new game every day. Her spontaneous play has found its way into this book in so many ways, and she enthusiastically offered her point of view as we developed ideas. Jeff Nisenoff also gave invaluable support in meeting some computer challenges as well as managing the important details of everyday life while this book came into being.

The Power of Games

• •

THE REMARKABLE POWER of games to engage our attention is evident all around us. Individually, and as a culture, we spend vast amounts of time, energy, and resources to watch and participate in games. Athletes are well-paid, stadiums are lavish, video games are ubiquitous, and school calendars are arranged to make sure that interschool sports can be accommodated. I'll bet that your cell phone even includes some tiny games so that you can play while waiting at the fast-food drive-up window. We are so awash in games every day that we may not even notice their abundance.

Basic principles of psychology tell us that anything done so often, by so many, must be motivating in its own right. There are all sorts of interesting theories about why games are motivating, but the bottom line is that there is something rewarding about games and that "something" is very powerful. It doesn't seem to be all about winning, either. Loyal fans of losing teams persevere as do gamblers who slip coin after coin in slot machines without a jackpot. Neither does that powerful "something" seem to demand that the game be easy to play. Multitudes of schoolchildren have memorized hundreds of complex character names, characteristics, and rules for fantasy video games, and they play tirelessly to move from level to level.

Let's face it, games are fun and fun is motivating. Along with food and shelter, fun is one of the basics of life people will seek. We will do something fun over and over again, just to have the experience. Things that are not fun will often be avoided, lied about, delegated to others, or generally shoved to the back of the closet—unless there is another payoff at the end of the drudgery, such as a paycheck or some boost to our personal status.

The fact is that most people willingly engage in difficult and even arduous tasks if those tasks are in the context of a game. This is the rationale for taking school skills and wrapping them up in some fun to harness the power of games for learning. The features that make some games fun and others dreary are tricky, but we know that people enjoy a challenge, some fair competition, an escape into another reality, and a bit of surprise, and so the games in the pages that follow contain those motivating features. Each game is an opportunity to bring playfulness to skill practice in a way that increases the "fun quotient" and fuels the desire to engage in the game again and again.

The games included here are obviously not video games and might be considered old-fashioned by some standards. But, remember, if you have never done it, it's new to you! So the novelty of these games for today's children is partly because they are three-dimensional, rather than on a flat screen. In fact, novelty is one of the things that makes a game fun and levels the playing field if you will, since no one in the room is likely to have ever "been there, done that" before. Other features that increase the fun quotient of these games are the unusual uses for common household items, the occasional possibility of having good luck beat skill, and the escape into an alternative reality with some rather quirky rules.

Just because something is motivating, used frequently, and valued in popular culture, doesn't mean that it should be endorsed in the classroom. Since we have a few other goals for schooling beyond the simple pursuit of fun and the thrill of winning, we have created these games to include the best aspects of the genre for use in supporting positive learning outcomes. *101 Great Classroom Games* is about fun with powerful, positive results.

Let the Games Begin!

· ·

EACH GAME IN this book is a "recipe for fun" with a purpose. If you are new to using games in the classroom, this book makes it easy to get started, but it is also designed to be useful for veteran gamers. The icons printed on each page provide a quick way to decide if the game includes the subject areas that you wish to reinforce. The games are rated for noise level to let you know if the game is quiet and calm enough for a learning center or better for an active setting. If a specific sort of game is desired, then the Grid Index to Games and the Skills Index to Games at the end of this book will be helpful in locating the activity that suits your purpose.

We understand all too well that classrooms are busy places and that teachers never seem to have enough time. With that in mind, many of these games use common school supplies and can be implemented with little preparation, and that is a great place to start if games are new for your class. For example, "Back Words" or "Shoebox" can be played while a group is waiting in a line, turning a fidgety transition time into an enjoyable bit of skill practice. These are just two instances of games actually making more time for learning, rather than taking time away from an already jam-packed day. Providing curriculum-relevant game materials at learning centers is an excellent way to engage students who finish other work early, and well-designed games can make "free choice" periods much more productive. It is all about making classroom time more relevant, productive, and engaging. This book is not about busywork!

Parent volunteers, assistants, and community businesses should not be overlooked as wonderful resources for pulling together materials to use in some of the games we have included. Since there are no expensive or exotic materials used in our games, a look through the garage or a junk drawer may be all that is needed to bring some fun to a day at school. Students themselves are also eager to bring in things to be used in a game they enjoy to make it more personalized. An example of this is found in "Pick a Pet," in which actual pet pictures can be included as game pieces. Even sets of game questions can be created by students for later use. This is a great help to the teacher, but also provides an extra opportunity for students to interact with significant subject matter before encountering it again in the game.

Each game in this book is written with a Setup section devoted to instructions for making the game components. We suggest that this section be copied and given to a willing volunteer. Then, the rules for playing the game are found separately in the How to Play Section so that they can be copied and put with the finished game if desired. How easy is that?

Now that we have addressed time constraints in the school day and limits on preparation time as potential obstacles to getting started with games, some educators may feel concerned about the psychological effects of competition and winning versus losing when games enter the classroom. These are not trivial concerns, especially for students with disadvantages and handicaps. With this in mind, most of our game designs include suggestions for variations to adjust for special concerns. There are also games played just for the enjoyment of the group outcome, such as "Who, What, When, Where, Why, and How?"

Our games can actually provide a venue for success that is not easily available in more conventional classroom tasks. Games offer the special combination of skill and a dash of good luck that can put the underdog in the winner's circle. Extra sensitivity to this factor can be noticed in the design of games with "instant win" sections on the boards and lucky rolls of the die that allow any player to make a big advance toward a win. We also suggest that younger players can continue with a game beyond the "first winner" to determine the "order of winners" so everyone can gain some sense of finishing, rather like the finish line of a race. Far from being unfair, these very aspects of playing make the game worth trying for someone normally less confident.

Anyone has a shot at winning. In this way, a game creates its own world in which all manner of outcomes are possible.

The other psychological benefit that games provide is their repeatability. There can always be a rematch! How about two out of three? This makes the winning and losing of individual games easier to accept and even leads to a greater desire to play again. (Remember that powerful "something" that keeps us playing?) As long as there is not a major tangible prize for just one winner on one play of the game, winning or losing is often just an invitation to play again. And, since everyone gets a chance to experience winning and losing sometime, better empathy and sportsmanship can develop through time.

Whether we love it or dread it, dealing with competition is a part of real life. This is not a reason to bring harsh, all-or-nothing battles into the childhood experience, but it is a reason to consider games for children as socially desirable. These games provide an emotional safety net for competition since it is "all in fun" anyhow. These playful chances to be beaten in the final play, misjudge your own abilities, or just plain make a mistake can help a player develop a resilient spirit to draw upon when these things inevitably happen "for real." Independent video game play simply cannot offer this significant benefit to character development. Play with people and play with machines are fundamentally different. In fact, there are few solitaire games in this collection precisely because learning happens best in a social setting. Plus, the games' shared reality and the need for players to agree on rule interpretation are a metaphor for serious real-world conflicts and negotiations. Seen in this light, the positive social outcomes of game play could be the most significant benefit to putting a little game board on a table in your room!

With all those potential obstacles out of the way, now is the time to wave the green flag and let the games begin!

ICONS KEY

 Language Arts

 General Fun

 Math

 Memory

 Social Studies

 **Strategy**

 Science

101 Great Classroom Games

General Fun Games for Any Subject

Bolt to the End

Teams collect points by answering questions and then use their points in a race to spin bolts along a rod.

Age Range: 9 to 12

Skills Used: factual knowledge, strategic thinking

Number of Players: 5 to 13

Noise Level: moderate to high

Activity Level: moderate

Materials: question-and-answer cards, stopwatch, threaded metal rods (2 feet each), thirty bolts, paint

Setup

The starting end of the threaded metal rods should be painted in a distinctive color to distinguish it from the finishing end, and the bolts should be checked to make sure they fit the rods and spin freely.

Question-and-answer cards should be prepared and given to the game director. Any single subject area or a combination of factual information can be used for the questions. For example: What is 7 × 8? (56); What is the capital of Wisconsin? (Madison); Who invented the lightbulb? (Thomas Edison); Spell the word *research*; What is the English translation for the Spanish word *gato*? (cat).

How to Play

This game is played in three parts. While all three parts can be played in one session, the final two parts would be fun to save for a culminating activity to a larger unit or enjoyed on a Friday afternoon. The event is something players will look forward to doing.

"Bolt to the End" is best played in teams of at least two players with an additional person designated as a game director. There can be as few as two teams or as many as four, if desired. For Part One of the game, each team determines an order of play within their group, similar to a batting order. Using a set of question-and-answer cards, the game director poses a question to the first player of the first team, then moves to the first player of the second team, and so on. Whenever a player answers correctly, that team keeps the card and scores one point. If the answer is incorrect, the card is placed back in the stack. Teams continue to answer questions until all the cards have been used or each team has had at least 10 turns. This part of the game ends with each team having a certain number of points.

In Part Two of the game, the team members decide how to "spend" their points. Points are exchanged for bolts and time limits. Each point can be exchanged for one bolt or 15 seconds of time. All teams must buy at least 15 seconds in order to participate in Part Three, but the final decision about exactly how many seconds and how many bolts to choose is a strategic decision. Exchange decisions should be done secretly. Teams will not know what their opponents have chosen until Part Three of the game.

Part Three uses a two-foot-long threaded rod and nuts that spin easily on it. The challenge is to move the metal nuts the entire length of the rod as quickly as possible. The team with the fewest bolts begins by placing all their bolts onto the rod. The bolts should be tight together and even with the starting end, which has been painted a distinctive color. The game director controls the stopwatch saying "Go" and "Stop" for whatever amount of time the team "bought" with their points from Part One. The teams work to move their bolts from the starting end of the rod all the way off the other end in the amount of time chosen. The final score is one point for each bolt all the way off the rod, with a five-point bonus for getting all the bolts off within the time limit.

The team with the next most bolts then takes up the challenge and so on. The team with the highest number of points from the bolt race is the ultimate winner.

Variation

■ This game can be exciting and fun when all teams are spinning their bolts at the same time. This variation can be done by stagger-ing the starts and having all teams finish at the same time. More supplies are needed, but the excitement of the finish can be worth it. A contest like this can be a bit noisy and is fun to watch, so it should be scheduled for a time when others nearby can take a break to watch.

Tips

■ Placing a towel under the rod is advisable to stop the bolts from bouncing out of sight on the floor after they are sent down the rod.

■ This game begs to be played more than once. Simple practice with the rods should be restricted in order to keep the game fresh and to keep teams from having too much expe-rience with how many bolts can be removed in a given time. Different positions of the rod and hand positions for spinning nuts can be decisive and add an interesting factor of chance and strategy to the game. These vari-ables are best discovered in a real play of the game so that the question-and-answer por-tion remains motivating.

Common Threads

Players are challenged to figure out the common characteristic or category for lists of three related items.

Age Range: 4 to 12

Skills Used: factual knowledge, reasoning, listening

Number of Players: 3 to 8

Noise Level: moderate to high

Activity Level: low

Materials: cards with lists of three related items

Setup

Create cards listing three items that have something in common. For example: hooves, paws, talons—kinds of feet; sash, cummerbund, belt—things that go around your waist; Ford, Allis Chalmers, John Deere—kinds of tractors; a hunter, Robin Hood, Cupid—all shoot a bow and arrow; and so on. Include the answer at the bottom or on the back of the card.

How to Play

The game director reads the list on the card and asks, "What's the common thread?" The players, or teams, quickly say their answer. The first correct answer is awarded a point. If two or more players answer at the same time, only those players are eligible to answer the next card to earn the point. Once the point has been given, everyone is back in the game. The player (or team) with the most points is the winner.

Variations

■ For younger or beginning players, make all of the items on the list belong to one category, such as triangle, circle, square (shapes) or red, yellow, blue (colors).

■ For slightly older players, make all of the items on the list have a similar characteristic, such as horses, lions, alligators (all have four legs) or grapes, pumpkins, cucumbers (all grow on vines).

■ For older or more advanced players, make sure the items sound dissimilar yet still have a common thread, such as tile, checkerboard, knot (all are square); a cherry, Edgar Allen Poe, an arm (all have pits); or a needle, a potato, a spider (all have eyes).

■ Let players take turns reading the list. The other players can write their answers. The reader verifies and awards a point to each person with the correct answer.

Tips

. . . .

■ Add more than three items to your lists for those just learning the game or if you want to reinforce certain vocabulary or characteristics.

■ Challenge players to think of additional groupings to use at another time.

■ Give credit to those who can think of another common thread for any given list.

■ Take the cards with you to play while waiting in line.

Fishy Facts

Using poles and hooks, players collect fish and add to their catch if they can successfully answer a question that is written on the side of the fish.

Age Range: 5 to 7
Skill Used: factual knowledge
Number of Players: 2 to 4
Noise Level: moderate
Activity Level: low
Materials: shallow box, such as a soda case box, painted blue; cutouts of fish; short "fishing pole" stick; paper clips; string

Setup

Using sturdy paper or tagboard, cut out 12 to 20 fish that are approximately 6 inches long with tails about 2 inches wide. Write a question on the body of the fish and write the answer on the tail. For example, write "2 + 6 =" on the body and "8" on the tail. The fish can also be prepared for learning paired information like foreign language translations, antonyms, or definitions of words. You can laminate the fish if you wish. On the back, tape a paper clip to the head of each fish so that from the front, only one loop of the clip shows.

Turn the box over so that the bottom becomes the top. Use a knife to cut twenty 2½-inch slits randomly in the box's surface. Slide the knife through each slit several times to make the slot wide enough to easily slide in the fish. Paint the box blue to make it look like water.

Get a small stick to use as the fishing pole. Attach a short string to the pole. For a hook, tie a paper clip that has been bent open at the end of the string.

Set up the game for play by sliding the fish—tail first—into various slots so the writing on the body of the fish faces the players.

How to Play

Players take turns choosing a fish to catch by reading or solving what is written on the fish's body. The player says his or her answer to the other players, hooks the fish, and then pulls it out with the fishing pole. If the answer on the fish matches what was said, the player keeps the fish and play goes to the next player. If the answer is different, the player slides the fish back into an available slot and it becomes the next player's turn. The game ends when all of the fish are caught or at the end of a set time. The player with the most fish is the winner.

Tips

■ Find art of a fish online or use an art software program. The art should be easy to cut out. Copy, paste, and resize the fish art in a document several times so you can print off a whole sheet of fish. If a color printer isn't available, run the pages off on different color paper for each skill.

■ Draw a wide blue line across the slits to make them very easy for the players to see when they are setting up the game. Decorate the edge of the box.

Get in Line

Players compete to put a set of cards in order, according to a characteristic, in the fastest time.

Age Range: 5 to 8
Skill Used: sequencing
Number of Players: 2 to 8
Noise Level: low to moderate
Activity Level: low
Materials: pack of cards for each player

Setup

For each player, prepare a pack of cards of items that can be put in sequence, such as numbers from 1 to 10; the alphabet; numbers counting by 2s, 5s, 10s; words to alphabetize; and so on.

How to Play

Each player takes a pack of the same type of cards. When all of the players have a pack, in unison they say, "1, 2, 3, get in line!" Each player tries to put his or her set of cards in the right order. When complete, the player announces, "I'm in line!" When everyone is finished, players compare sequences. Play multiple times until a player is the fastest three times. That player is the winner.

Variations

■ Play in teams with no talking. Signaling is okay. Everyone on the team must agree with the sequence before they can say, "We're in line!"

■ Award points as players finish their sequence. If there are four players, the first one done receives four points, the second one gets three points, the third one earns two points, and the final player gets one point. Keep track of points earned during the time of play.

■ Flip a coin with heads being "high" and tails being "low" prior to sequencing the cards. If heads (high) is flipped, players will sort the cards from high to low and vice versa.

Tips

■ Let younger players take a token each time they are the fastest to help them remember how many rounds they have won.

■ Place packs of matching cards in a plastic self-sealing bag. Label the bag with the skill and the number of packs.

Hide and Seeds

Players shake and roll a jar in an effort to find the items lurking in the seeds. Once spotted, the items are checked off a list.

Age Range: 4 to 12
Skills Used: visual discrimination, reading, record keeping
Number of Players: 2 to 6
Noise Level: moderate
Activity Level: low
Materials: clear plastic jar with a secure lid, small toys and objects, birdseed, timer, game sheet

Setup

Various objects and small toys are used for this game. They can be related to a particular theme or subject of study. For a dinosaur theme, for example, the objects might include toy dinosaurs, archaeological tools (brush and small hammer), bone models, a plastic egg, and a bit of silk fern. A list of the objects is written on a game sheet, which also includes spaces for checking off the items as they are discovered. Once the items have been placed in the jar, the remaining space is filled with birdseed, leaving an inch or so of empty space so that the seeds will move around enough to reveal the hidden objects.

How to Play

This game is best played as a cooperative activity with a group attempting to uncover as many items on the game sheet as they can within a specified time limit. The timer is started, and the group begins manipulating the jar. As each item is found, it is checked off the sheet. If desired, teams can compete to find a greater number of items than the first group given the same time limit.

Variations

■ This game can be changed to fit different holidays and units of study simply by changing the items that are hidden in the seeds. For a unit on space exploration, for example, the toys can be rockets, astronauts, star-shaped beads, foam moon shapes, space program patches, and planet models.

■ A more difficult task is introduced to the game if alphabet beads are placed on bits of pipe cleaner to spell words that fit the theme of the jar. For the variation above, for example, the beads could spell out *"Apollo 13"* or use number beads for "1969" as a reference to the first moon landing.

■ A further challenge can be added by asking players to make a list of the objects that they locate. Lists then can be compared among groups to see which team has located the most items within the time limit.

Tips

■ The jar used for this activity must be clear plastic. The size of the jar can make the game easier or harder as desired. Larger and wider jars have more hidden space and are more challenging. The shapes of certain objects make them extremely difficult to find in this game as well. If the object fills with seeds at one end, for example, that heavier part will tend to stay hidden in the center of the jar and only the lighter parts will protrude from the seeds. Objects that are the same color as the seeds will also be much more difficult to locate.

■ If you believe that your players will resort to opening the container to discover the contents, it might be advisable to use sturdy tape to secure the lid. For some groups, the warning "Do Not Open" written on the cover might be enough. A floor full of birdseed is not a good ending for this game! Gluing the top on the jar is not suggested as it does not allow the game to be changed as desired to use again and again.

■ Be sure to make a comprehensive list of the objects in the jar before pouring in the birdseed. Once hidden, it can be very hard to remember the items or find them again to create the list.

■ Using several similar items with color variations is a way to add complexity to the game or increase the number of target items, if desired.

■ Players can be asked to contribute items for the game in advance of the setup to add some interest to the activity. These can be returned after the game is recycled to another version.

Pick a Pet

Players answer questions and roll a die to collect pet supplies and ultimately "pick a pet."

Age Range: 5 to 9
Skills Used: pet care knowledge, factual knowledge
Number of Players: 2 to 6
Noise Level: moderate
Activity Level: low
Materials: pictures of pets and pet supplies, die, question-and-answer cards, game key

Setup

The game pieces for "Pick a Pet" are laminated pictures of pets and their supplies. For each pet represented in the game, there should be a picture appropriate for each of the following categories that will correspond to values on the die: 1—habitat, 2—food and water, 3—exercise and play, 4—a special item specific to that pet, 5—a vet, and 6—a picture of the pet itself. Suggested pets are cat, dog, horse, fish, mouse, and bird. The pictures do not need to be in scale with each other to be used for this game.

"Special items" for the six pets listed above could include:

Cat—scratching post
Dog—leash and collar
Horse—saddle
Fish—tank light
Mouse—chewing stick
Bird—cuttlebone

"Toys" for the six pets could include:

Cat—feathered ball
Dog—bone or tennis ball
Horse—fence to jump
Fish—aquarium cave or treasure chest
Mouse—exercise wheel
Bird—bell or mirror

Game cards should be prepared with a question or prompt on one side and the answer on the reverse. This format allows for self-checking as players participate in the game. The content of the questions can suit most any subject, but all cards for the game should address the same area. Various subject examples include: A spider is an insect—true or false? (false); On which continent is Egypt? (Africa); 6 + __ = 10. (4). There should be at least six cards per player.

How to Play

The question-and-answer cards are shuffled and placed on the table with the question side up. The player who is chosen to go first answers the question on the top card. If correct, that player rolls the die that corresponds with a picture category as shown in the game key. A roll of 1 allows that player to choose a habitat and get started collecting the remaining pictures. If the roll is 2 through 6, no picture is chosen and the next player takes a turn.

Once a player has obtained a habitat, he or she can begin to collect supplies by choosing items after rolling a 2, 3, 4, or 5 in any order, according to the key. (A roll of 6 in this part of the game results in a lost turn because the player doesn't have all the supplies needed to be ready to "pick a pet.") For example, a roll of 3 allows the player to take an item meant for exercise or playing with a pet. Players are not required to take items that correspond to any particular pet. Mixing items may upset some players, but most will enjoy the silliness of putting an exercise wheel in a stable or a saddle on a fish. When all the supplies have been collected on various turns, players must roll a 6 to take the pet picture of their choice. Any other roll results in a loss of a turn. The first player to "pick a pet" is the winner.

Variation

■ Adjust the difficulty level of this game by choosing or creating an appropriate set of question-and-answer cards. These should not be so difficult that players seldom get to roll the die. The cards could be omitted completely for the youngest players. In this case, they would simply roll the die on each turn.

Tips

■ Magazines and pet catalogs are good sources for pictures of pets and pet supplies. Your local pet store would probably allow you take digital pictures of their pets and supplies. Players can also be asked to bring in photos of their own pets and supplies. A mixture of these resources can be used to obtain enough pictures to play this game.

■ It is helpful to laminate each category of picture with a uniquely colored border to make game play easier. For example, all habitat pictures can be glued to yellow cardstock that extends beyond the edge of the picture before laminating. Pictures need not match in size.

■ A copy of the game key should be provided during the game. Use the key provided, or make your own. Include the category, the color of the picture border (if used), and the value of the die. For example, the key could show "Habitat—yellow—1," "Food and water—blue—2," and so on.

1	Habitat
2	Food & Water
3	Exercise & Play
4	Special Item
5	Vet
6	Pet Picture

Pop a Wheelie

Players assemble pictures of bike riders by rolling a die and answering questions.

Age Range: 7 to 12
Skill Used: factual knowledge
Number of Players: 2 to 4
Noise Level: moderate
Activity Level: low
Materials: bike pictures, die, question-and-answer cards, game key

Setup

This game uses full side-view pictures of riders on bikes. A full picture is needed for each player of the game and it is more interesting if the pictures do not match each other. To prepare the game pieces, the pictures should be laminated and cut into parts. Each picture should be cut into seven pieces that show these elements: two separate wheels, frame, seat, handlebars, pedals, and rider wearing a helmet.

Use the game key provided or prepare a key that tells which bike parts correspond to the values on the die. These are: 1 for wheels, 2 for frame, 3 for seat, 4 for handlebars, 5 for pedals, and 6 for rider. Question-and-answer cards should be chosen and shuffled in preparation for the game as well; they are useful for self-checking during game play. Almost any subject area can be used to create a set of game cards. For example: What are the three states of matter? (gas, liquid, and solid); What is the opposite of dilatory? (punctual).

How to Play

To play the game, all the picture pieces are spread out on the table in full view and the game key is displayed. The player chosen to go first takes a card and answers the question. If the answer is correct, the player rolls the die. A roll of 1, called a "wheelie," must be earned first to start the picture. Once a player has the first wheel, the frame must be added next. Then the other wheel, handlebars, and pedals can be added in any order. The rider is earned last. If any player answers incorrectly, he or she doesn't get to roll and play passes to the left. If a player already has the piece designated by his or her roll, he or she passes and loses a turn. The game ends when a player adds the rider to complete a picture, winning the game.

Tips

■ Popular biking magazines and bike catalogs from bike shops can be a source for appealing pictures of stunt bikers. Players can be asked to contribute pictures from their own magazines for use in making this game. Or for a personalized game, players can have digital pictures of themselves taken on their own bikes to be used as game pieces.

■ Mount each set of pictures on a different color to help in selecting pieces from the same picture if desired, but mixing up the picture parts can make the game more fun and could be allowed.

Pop a Wheelie Game Key

1	**Wheels**
2	**Frame**
3	**Seat**
4	**Handlebars**
5	**Pedals**
6	**Rider**

■ **Earn a wheel first.**

■ **Then add a frame.**

■ **Add another wheel, the seat, the handlebars, and the pedals in any order.**

■ **Get the rider last.**

Rubber-Band Rodeo

Rubber bands round up corresponding pairs of items, and the player with the most correct matches wins.

Age Range: 5 to 10

Skills Used: matching, factual knowledge

Number of Players: 2

Noise Level: low

Activity Level: low

Materials: game board, 20 rubber bands (10 each of two colors)

Setup

Copy and use the sample game board provided or create game boards having four columns. Make the inner two columns half the width of the outer columns. Divide the columns into an even number of rows. In the wider outer columns, create a matching activity by filling in words with definitions, equations with answers, pictures matching vocabulary words, pictures corresponding to initial or ending consonants, states and their capitals, and so on. Be sure that the matching answers are not all next to each other on the game board, but randomly ordered in adjacent columns.

Draw a dot in the middle of each space in the narrow columns. Put a paper fastener through each dot. Loop rubber bands around the paper fasteners to match each pair yourself and then draw lines on the back of the game board so players can self-check their answers.

How to Play

Each player selects his or her color of rubber band to use for this game. Players take turns matching the pairs of items in the cowboy and calf columns. If players disagree with an answer, they can use one of their rubber bands to lasso a calf that has already been roped.

When all of the items have been matched, players check their answers using the back of the game board. The person with the most calves correctly lassoed is the winner.

Tips

■ Add cowboy or western graphics to each game board.

■ Make an extra copy of the game board, cutting off the outside columns so only the Cowboy and Calf columns remain. Draw the correct roping pattern. Store this in a pocket on the back of the game board. At the end of the game, players can lay the answer strip on the completed game board to check their answers. If you use this method and have more than one of these game boards in your classroom at a time, be sure to label the answer strip so it can be matched with the proper game board in case pieces get mixed up.

Rubber-Band Rodeo Game Board

	Cowboy	Calf	
	●	●	
	●	●	
	●	●	
	●	●	
	●	●	
	●	●	
	●	●	
	●	●	
	●	●	

Which One?

Players move to separate parts of the room to show their preferences.

Age Range: 4 to 12
Skills Used: listening, self-evaluation
Number of Players: 2 to 30
Noise Level: moderate to high
Activity Level: high
Materials: list of fun "choice" questions

Setup

A list of questions is prepared for this game to provide fun choices to evaluate. They do not have to be opposites to be interesting. Select questions with abstract preferences in this format: "Are you _____ or _____?" Avoid pairings with a perceived "good" or "bad" choice. An example with an abstract preference is "Are you math or reading?" Other sample questions include:

Are you . . .

mountain or valley?
ocean or lake?
cat or dog?
music or art?
glove or mitten?
bike or skateboard?
day or night?
hot or cold?
loud or quiet?
bird or fish?
hamburger or hot dog?
paper or plastic?

movie or play?
concert or museum?
orange or purple?
fancy or plain?
big or small?
tree or flower?
boot or sandal?
snow or sand?
inside or outside?

How to Play

This game is best played in a large room in which some running is allowed. One person is designated as the game director and is positioned in a central location. Two different parts of the room are chosen as destinations for the players. The game begins with all players in the center of the room with the game director.

The questions pose two choices for the players and they "vote with their feet" to show their preference, going to the side of the room with the other players who make the same choice that they do. The game director points to the opposite sides of the room as the parts of the question are given and no one moves until both choices are read.

Variations

■ This game can be played with two people who both read the question and share their answers quietly with each other.

■ Several pairs can do this at the same time and record their number of "same" and "different" choices to compare with other pairs.

■ If a question results in a single person in one of the two groups, that person is given the chance to be the game director.

■ The game director can "freeze" the groups at any time if two teams are needed for any other activity or game.

■ Questions should be written ahead of time to avoid offering a choice with double meanings or potentially offensive interpretations.

Tips

■ This is a good game to relieve excess energy while exercising some self-awareness and group awareness.

Who Am I?

Players wear cards on their foreheads and ask yes and no questions to discover what is written there.

Age Range: 9 to 12
Skills Used: reasoning, factual knowledge
Number of Players: 6 to 25
Noise Level: moderate
Activity Level: high
Materials: elastic headbands for each player, identity cards

Setup

Elastic headbands are needed to play this game. There should be one for every player. Pertinent identities are written on cards. These should relate to a particular theme or subject area and do not have to be people, but can also be things, places, occupations, or animals, if desired. Examples of identities related to occupations could include: dentist, firefighter, airline pilot, teacher, nurse, and truck driver. For a game revolving around a specific theme like the solar system, the identities could include: sun, asteroid, comet, Earth, Saturn, and Mercury. A different identity card is needed for each player.

How to Play

This game is a variation on the classic 20 Questions game. In this version, each player wears a headband so that it crosses his or her forehead. The game director places an identity card in each player's headband while keeping it hidden from the person wearing it. The card faces outward so everyone else can read it.

Players circulate freely through the room asking yes or no questions of other players until correctly determining their own identity. Once the player guesses correctly, the card is removed from the band and the player continues to circulate and provide answers to others.

Tips

■ Announce the theme or topic of the cards to help focus players' questions.

■ This game can be a good icebreaker for a group if a theme is revealed and the identities are common knowledge for players. An animal theme would be appropriate for younger players. Occupations could correspond with a study of careers. Older players might be challenged to guess famous figures from the American Revolution.

■ If players are too self-conscious to wear headbands, then the game can be modified to have the cards taped on their backs until they guess correctly. The headband version of the game lends itself to a more playful atmosphere and will be noisier to play.

Language Arts Games

Back Words

Teams compete in a relay race by drawing letters on each other's backs as a means of passing along a target word to the farthest person in line.

Age Range: 8 to 10
Skills Used: reading, memory
Number of Players: 6 to 10
Noise Level: moderate
Activity Level: moderate
Materials: word cards

Setup

Common words of three, four, and five letters are written on cards. It is helpful to separate the cards into different stacks based on the number of letters.

How to Play

This game is played with two teams of equal size. Players line up behind—but within reach—of each other. They can be sitting or standing. Play starts with the player at the back of each line being given a three-letter word written on a card. The challenge is to write that word, letter by letter, on the back of the person ahead of him or her. The player continues to write the word until the receiving player signals, "Got it!" Then that player writes the word in the same fashion on the back of the next player. Play continues along the line to the front person.

The first front player to say, "Got it!" can win for his or her team if that player says the right word. If the word is correct, that team scores one point, but if the guess is wrong, the other team scores the point.

The front players go to the back of their respective lines for the second round. Teams continue to move players at the front of the line to the starting spot in this manner until each player has had the same number of turns in that position (i.e., six rounds for teams of three). The team with the most points wins the game. The game director can increase the challenge by giving words of four or five letters, but each team should have the same length word on each round.

Variation

■ A noncompetitive version of this game can be played with players in a circle to bring the word back to the person who started the chain to see if the word can be preserved through several interpretations.

Tips

■ Some age groups might be more comfortable with teams being all girls or all boys since the game involves physical contact. If this is not feasible, the game can be modified to have players write with their fingers in the palm of the next player's hand.

■ This game can be played for fun while a group is waiting in a line. It offers the benefit that the last person in line actually has an advantage rather than feeling unfortunate.

Basewordball

Teams score home runs by identifying base words.

Age Range: 8 to 11
Skill Used: knowledge of prefixes, suffixes, base/root words
Number of Players: 8 to 24
Noise Level: moderate to high
Activity Level: moderate to high
Materials: pack of prefix and/or suffix cards, die, four bases, chart paper, game key, game board (optional)

Setup

Use the sample prefix/suffix cards provided or write prefixes and suffixes on separate cards to make a deck of about 30 cards. Prefixes and suffixes can be repeated within the deck.

Place the bases on the floor, arranged in a diamond shape as in a baseball game.

How to Play

Players are divided into two teams. The pitching team selects a pitcher to draw and read the prefix or suffix cards and a catcher who writes the opposing team's words on the chart paper. The player who is first in the batting order for the hitting team listens to the prefix or suffix "pitched" to him or her and tries to say and spell a word containing it. For example, the pitcher says, "-ly." The hitter could say, "*Slowly*, s-l-o-w-l-y." The catcher writes the word with the given spelling on the chart paper. If the word uses the prefix or suf-

fix correctly and is spelled correctly, the batter rolls the die and follows the directions that go with the number on the game key. The batter is out if the prefix or suffix is used incorrectly or the word is not spelled correctly. If a word is reused, the batter is automatically out.

The game continues with players advancing around the bases to score runs until three players are "out" and the teams exchange positions. A predetermined number of innings can be played with the highest scoring team winning the game.

Variation

■ Cards could contain a word with a prefix, suffix, or both. The batting team would have to identify and spell the base/root word correctly in order to roll the die to move.

Tips

■ Have the pitching team change pitchers and catchers each inning so more players have the opportunity of reading the cards and writing the words.

■ If there isn't room to physically have bases and players moving around the room, copy and use the baseball diamond game board provided here. Players can then use game tokens to move around the bases. Another option is to make a baseball diamond poster with hook and loop tape on the bases and markers that can be moved from base to base.

Basewordball Prefix/Suffix Cards

dis___	un___	___ful
un___	re___	___ness
re___	dis___	___ly
de___	un___	___an
im___	___ing	___ist
mis___	___ed	___er
semi___	___ly	___est
non___	___er	___less
re___	___est	___ful
dis___	___less	___ness

Basewordball Key

1	**Single—move one base**
2	**Double—move two bases**
3	**Triple—move three bases**
4	**Home Run!**
5	**Foul Ball—take another turn**
6	**Caught Ball—you're out!**

Basewordball Game Board

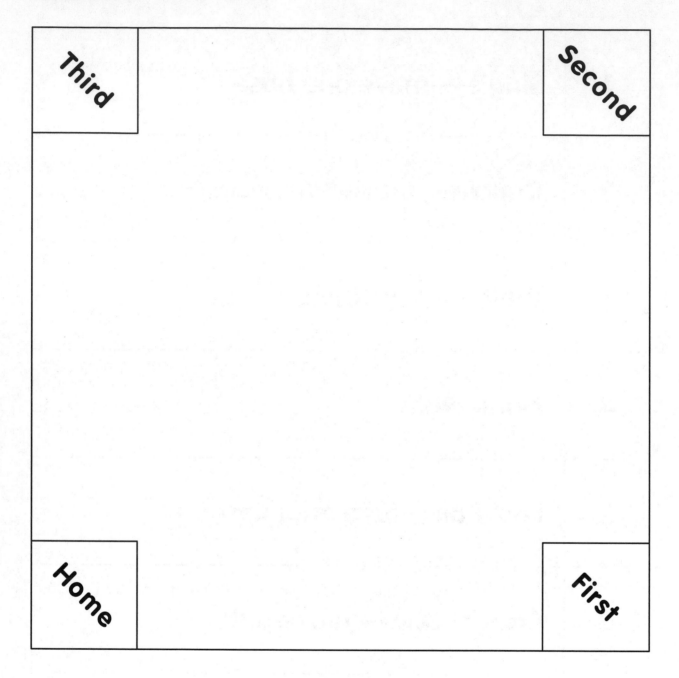

Black Out

Players strategically choose five words from a designated page in a book and cross out letters as they are randomly chosen from a bag.

Age Range: 7 to 11
Skill Used: key word recognition
Number of Players: 2 to 24
Noise Level: low to moderate
Activity Level: low
Materials: set of books (enough for each player to have the same one); letter cards in a cloth bag; pencil and paper

Setup

Make cards with the letters of the alphabet or use alphabet tiles or magnetic letters. Be sure there is only one of each letter. Place the letters in the bag.

How to Play

The player selected to go first chooses a page and all the others open their books to the same spot. Using that page, each player chooses five words from the text and writes them on a sheet of paper. The one who chose the page draws letters, one at a time, from the bag and announces the letter to the other players. Players cross out that letter every time it appears in all of their words. When all of the letters on his or her sheet are crossed out, that person says, "Black out" and is out of the game. The winner is the last person with letters not yet crossed out.

Variation

■ Instead of a set of identical books, the words can be chosen from a handout, such as a spelling list, science vocabulary sheet, or poetry selection. The written material could also be projected on a screen while players choose their target words.

Tip

■ Have the winner share the strategy he or she used to help him or her win. Winning strategies might be to select words with few common consonants or to choose long words.

Box Top Tops

Players spin tops to select overused adjectives and supply fresh descriptors. The first one to offer synonyms for his or her six target words is the winner.

Age Range: 7 to 11

Skill Used: synonym knowledge

Number of Players: 2 to 6

Noise Level: moderate

Activity Level: low

Materials: 12″ × 18″ gift box top marked into sections, individual game sheets, small toy tops, paper and pencil

Setup

The game is played with toy tops in the lid of an ordinary shirt-sized gift box. The tops should be simple plastic or wooden toys that work with a twist of the fingers rather than elaborate ones using a string mechanism. Players can either share one top to play the game, or each player can have a top.

The box top should have 10 to 12 sections drawn on it in the style of a crazy quilt, as shown in the sample. The spaces do not need to be the same size or shape, but they should be large enough to have a top fit into it when it comes to rest. A word is written in each space before the game. The words written in the spaces should be mundane adjectives that are familiar and overused such as *nice, good, bad, big, small, hot, cold, fast, slow, pretty, ugly, amazing,* and *tired.*

How to Play

Players choose six words found on the box top and write them in the spaces on their game sheet. When all players have written their words, the game sheets are passed to the left to be used by the player next to them for the remainder of the game.

The player who is selected to go first spins a top in the box. The top should land on a word section. If it seems to land evenly across two or more spaces, then the player spins again. If the word under the top appears on the player's word list, he or she offers a synonym for the overused word and writes it on the list. The game continues in the same manner for the next players, but no one may write down a word that has already been used by another player as an answer. The first player to have synonyms written for all six of his or her words is the winner. The remaining players can continue playing until each person has finished the game.

Variations

■ This game can be modified to include any set of overused words. For example, a verb version of this game could include words such as *said* and *went.*

■ Instead of words, numbers can be written on the box top and players can try to land on answers to number facts on their particular game boards.

■ Players can be asked to come up with a rhyming word for the one written in the box top section.

■ Younger players could be challenged to think of a word that starts with a particular letter. A variety of letters would be written in the box top spaces for this form of the game.

Box Top Tops Game Sheet

Game Board Words						Synonym

Game Board Words						Synonym

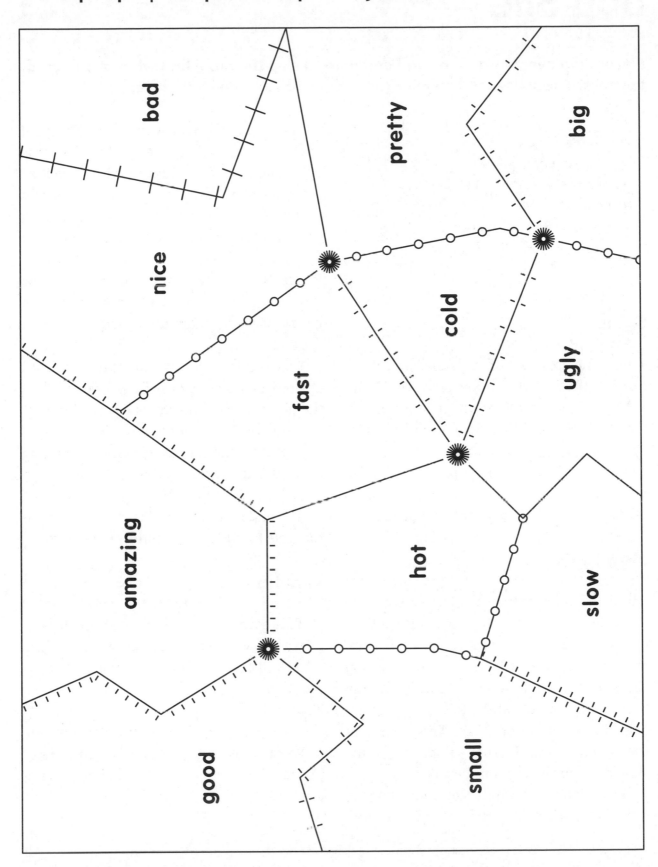

Bug Bite

Players flip over word cards and compete to slap the table first when a bug card appears. The successful slapper reads the word and collects the card.

Age Range: 5 to 8
Skill Used: reading
Number of Players: 2 to 4
Noise Level: moderate to high
Activity Level: low to moderate
Materials: set of word/bug cards

Setup

This game uses a set of cards that all look the same on the back. The fronts of the cards have either familiar words or pictures of bugs on them. There should be about 6 word cards for every bug card in the deck, and there should be about 15 cards available per player. For example, two players would need a deck of about 30 cards with at least 5 bug cards included.

How to Play

All of the cards are shuffled and dealt facedown to the players. The players leave their cards in a facedown stack in front of them. To begin the game, players turn over the top cards of their decks simultaneously, putting them in the middle of the table where everyone can see and reach them. This is done as the players chant, "Hornet, wasp, bee." Cards should be turned over on the word *bee*.

Play continues with the cards stacking up, until a card with a bug on it appears. The first player to slap the bug with his or her hand and say, "Bug bite!" gets to read all the cards on the table. Cards read correctly are kept by that player, and the other cards are returned to the center pile to await the next bug card. The bug card is also collected as long as at least one word is correctly read. The bug card is shuffled into the player's card stack to turn up again. The correctly read cards are set aside by the player who captured them to score at the end.

Play continues in the same manner until any one player runs out of word cards. Then the game is over and the one with the most captured cards, including bug cards, wins.

A player who slaps when there is no bug is penalized one card and must put it back in the pile to be slapped. If two players slap side by side at the same time, the cards are left on the table for the next slapping opportunity.

Variation

■ This game can be played with math facts instead of word cards. Players would collect cards by correctly solving equations.

Tip

■ Word cards can be duplicates and might include sight words or important new vocabulary words.

Character Guess

Players compete to guess the name of a fictional character after hearing the fewest hints. More and more obvious hints, worth fewer points, are given until everyone knows the answer.

Age Range: 6 to 12
Skills Used: memory, story comprehension, reasoning
Number of Players: 2 to 8
Noise Level: low
Activity Level: low
Materials: character cards

Setup

Keep a list of main characters familiar to the players. As that list is developed, add some key descriptors for each character, such as had three sisters, lived in Portland, was captured by two boys, and so on. Using the Character Guess card form provided, write the 10 descriptors from least evident to almost telling the character's name. For example, a 10-descriptor list for Cinderella might be:

10 points—Lived happily ever after
9 points—Dreamed as she worked
8 points—Was friends with mice and a rat
7 points—Rode in a coach
6 points—Danced with a prince
5 points—Had a fairy godmother
4 points—Didn't want to hear the clock strike 12
3 points—Had wicked stepsisters
2 points—Wore a glass slipper
1 point—Was made to live in cinders

How to Play

Each player starts with 10 points. The game director reads the clue worth 10 points first. If the players have an answer, they write it on their response sheets and hide it with their hands. The game director peeks and if the answer is correct, the player gets a thumbs-up sign. Those with the correct answer earn 10 points. The game director continues reading the clues in order and checking after each. As the players come up with the answer, they earn the corresponding number of points. The person with the most points after several rounds is the winner.

Variations

■ Sets of clues can be written for other categories such as states, famous people, or historic places.

■ A unit of study can be targeted and each round could be identified as a person, place, or thing having to do with that particular subject.

Tips

· ·

■ Have each student select a favorite character and write 5 to 10 clues, depending on age or skill level. Play with these as a culminating activity for the unit.

■ Play in teams against other classes who are using the same stories or studying the same subjects.

Character Guess Card

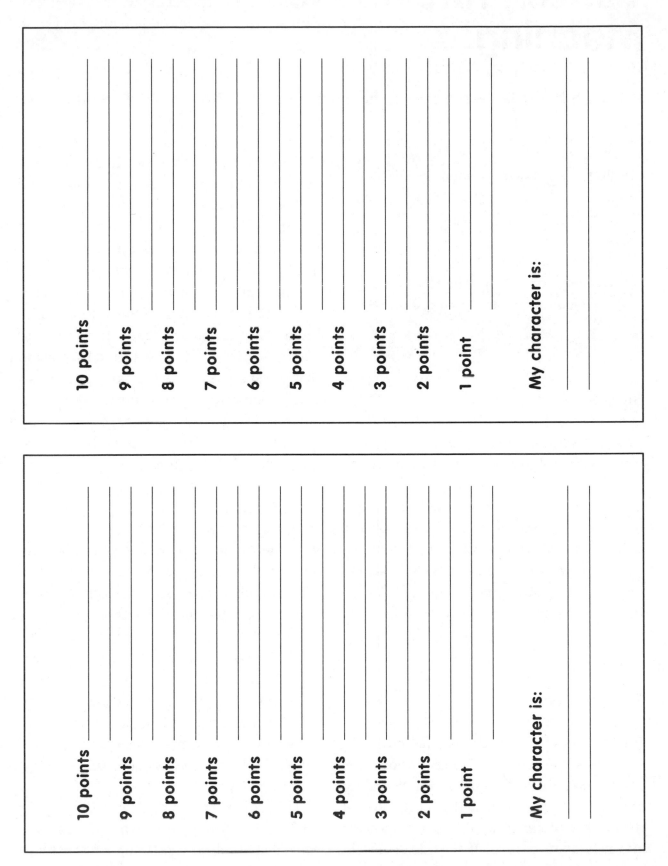

10 points _____

9 points _____

8 points _____

7 points _____

6 points _____

5 points _____

4 points _____

3 points _____

2 points _____

1 point _____

My character is: _____

10 points _____

9 points _____

8 points _____

7 points _____

6 points _____

5 points _____

4 points _____

3 points _____

2 points _____

1 point _____

My character is: _____

Concentrate on the Meaning

Players turn cards over to match the most words with their multiple definitions.

Age Range: 7 to 10

Skill Used: knowledge of multiple-meaning words

Number of Players: 2

Noise Level: low

Activity Level: low

Materials: sets of three cards (one word card and two corresponding definition cards)

Setup

Create several three-card sets that involve words with multiple meanings that are appropriate to the skill level of the players. On one card in the set, write a word that has multiple meanings. On the other two cards, write a different definition that corresponds with the word. For example, on one card write *bat*. On one definition card, write "a type of stick used in baseball" and on the other card write "a flying mammal." At least eight sets are needed for the game.

How to Play

Players spread the cards out, facedown, in even rows and columns Concentration-style. Players take turns turning over and reading two cards. If a word card and a definition card match, the player picks up those two cards and gets another turn. If they don't match,

the cards are turned facedown and it becomes the other player's turn. If two definition cards are selected, the player turns them back over and loses a turn.

Since there will be a definition card remaining facedown after a match, anytime during the game on his or her turn, a player has the option of turning up just one card to find the second definition card for one of his or her previous matches. If the second definition card is found, that card is added to that player's pile. If a word card rather than a definition card is turned up, the player can attempt to find a definition for that word.

The winner is the player with the most cards after a set time limit.

Variations

■ Content or general knowledge can be reinforced with this game. Make sets of three cards on other topics such as earth features with specific examples of each, for example, mountain, Mount Rainier, Mount McKinley; river, Mississippi River, Nile River; and so on. Another option is to use names of various animals such as rooster, hen, chick and ram, ewe, lamb. Or, use animal classification and animals from that group such as mammal, bat, whale; bird, eagle, penguin; and so on.

■ This can turn into a math game by making cards with a number and two equations that equal that number. Another option is to make cards with three forms of a number such as 23, 2 tens and 3 ones, 20 + 3, or twenty-three; 147, 100 + 40 + 7, one hundred forty-seven; and so on.

Tips

■ To aid the players in laying out the cards, make a game board showing the layout of the cards. Trace a pattern of the card for each space so the cards can easily be put in place.

■ To speed up the game and to aid memory of the placement of the cards, use a certain symbol or color on the backs of the word cards and another symbol or color for the backs of the definition cards.

Cross Out

Players write three words relating to a given category and then cross out letters one at a time. The last player with a letter showing wins.

Age Range: 7 to 12
Skills Used: categorizing, vocabulary knowledge
Number of Players: 2 to 8
Noise Level: low
Activity Level: low
Materials: category cards, pencil and paper

Setup

Make a pack of category cards. Categories could be general things, such as flowers, mammals, and cities, or more specific items, such as cold places, animals that live underground, things with four wheels, candy that is individually wrapped, and sports played with a round ball.

How to Play

A game director is chosen who draws a category card and reads it out loud. Each player writes three words that go with that category. As the players are doing that, the game director writes the alphabet on the board. Then, players take turns saying a letter of the alphabet. After a letter is selected, the players cross out that letter in all of their words and the game director crosses the letter out on the board. Players should have an equal number of turns selecting letters until there are fewer than eight left. After all of the turns, the player with the most letters left is the winner.

Tips

■ Encourage players to use dictionaries, textbooks, or brainstormed word lists to develop their three-word lists.

■ If playing as a large group or class, set a time for when the game will be played so players can use free time to choose the three words for their lists. After the game, let the winner share his or her strategy for having the most letters remaining.

■ Make a deck of alphabet cards or put a set of alphabet tiles in a bag. Have players draw a letter card or tile to make the game's outcome random.

■ Words can be checked for spelling and correct categorization before the letter calling begins.

Dipping and Dripping Rhymes

Players soak nonsense word cards in water to reveal a target word to rhyme.

Age Range: 7 to 10
Skills Used: reading, rhyming
Number of Players: 2 to 6
Noise Level: moderate
Activity Level: moderate
Materials: hidden word cards, markers (permanent and washable), bowls of water, paper and pencils, paper towels

Setup

This game requires advance preparation of cards with hidden words on them. The target words are written on the cards in permanent ink with random-sized spaces between the letters. The spaces between the target word's letters are filled with distracting letters written in matching washable ink. For example, the word *cat* might appear on the card as *bocrutangetable*. Any number of distracting letters can be added to the target word, including letters that are in the target word. There should be enough of these cards prepared so that each player can have at least four.

Each player should have a cereal bowl with about an inch of water in it. The bowls should be large enough to allow the word cards to lie fairly flat at the bottom and get completely wet. Paper towels, paper, and a pencil for each player are also needed.

How to Play

Play begins with all the cards faceup spread on the table. Players take turns choosing one card from the array. When each person has a card, a signal is given for players to place their cards in the water. The letters written in washable marker will begin to fade as the card is agitated in the water. As soon as a player can read the target word, he or she should write down as many rhyming words as possible. There is no time limit for this part of the game, and there is no need to do this secretly because each person will have a different target word.

When all players have exhausted their ideas, the results are shared. Incorrect rhymes are crossed out, and the number of correct rhymes is tallied to complete a round of play.

Once dunked, the word card should be removed from the bowl and placed on the paper towel to dry. Another card is selected by each player for a second round and play continues until all the cards have been used. The number of correct words written in each round is added up by each player, with the highest total for all rounds determining the game winner.

Variation

■ To change this game into a synonym game, the target words can be overused words such as *nice* and *big.* The task would then be to write a list of synonyms for the target word revealed when the card is soaked in the water.

Tips

■ Test some markers to find a pair of permanent and washable markers that give a similar line on the paper. It is important for the letters to be indistinguishable before the nonsense word is dipped in the water.

■ Players will typically want to continue dipping the cards to discover the words until all the cards are used, so only the desired number of cards should be available.

■ A timer is not necessary. There should be a natural conclusion to the rounds, and players with easier words should get the benefit of the time to write all the answers they can generate.

Don't Say "It"

Players give spontaneous one-minute speeches on randomly drawn everyday topics while trying to avoid saying a designated "poison word."

Age Range: 8 to 12
Skills Used: listening, verbal expression
Number of Players: 2 to 6
Noise Level: moderate to high
Activity Level: moderate
Materials: stopwatch, topic cards, die, game key

Setup

A set of cards for this game should be prepared with topics of conversation that are appropriate for the age group playing the game. Use the sample topic cards provided here, or create your own.

A list of prohibited words for the game needs to be chosen prior to starting the game. This list should include the word *it* so that the name of the game makes sense, but up to five other words might be chosen to suit the group. Some suggestions are *you, thing, like, I,* and *well*. These six words can be written on an oversized foam die or copy and complete the sample key so that players can use a regular die.

How to Play

To begin a turn, a player draws a topic card and rolls the die to determine the "poison word"—the word he or she is not allowed to say. The topic and poison word are told to all the other players before the speech starts. A start signal is given by a player holding the stopwatch and the speaker is timed for one minute. The challenge is to continue speaking for that minute while avoiding the poison word. Anyone who hears the poison word can call attention to it and the speaker is out of the game. Players are also disqualified if they are silent for 15 seconds or more during their minute. This time limit can be enforced by the player with the stopwatch or an additional stopwatch can be used. At the end of a minute, a signal is given and the speaker can stop at that moment, without finishing a sentence or thought.

Rounds continue with players speaking on different topics with various poison words each time, depending on the card chosen and roll of the die. Successful speakers advance to the next round, until only one player is left as the winner. If two or more players fail in the final round, they each get another turn until one player truly outperforms the others and wins.

Variation

■ Choosing *um* and *ah* as possible poison words makes this game very difficult since these are extremely hard to avoid in spontaneous speech. If this variation is used, it is suggested that all players have the same poison word in any given round, even though the topics might be different.

Tip

■ Having the group brainstorm subjects for the topic cards can make this game more fun for the players.

Die	"Poison" Word
1	it
2	
3	
4	
5	
6	

Don't Say "It" Sample Cards

Explain how to make a pizza.	Explain how to whistle.
Describe an airplane.	Tell what you had for breakfast.
Describe fireworks.	Tell how to mail a letter.
Explain the rules of baseball.	Tell how to plant a tree.
List the things in your locker.	Describe the smell of the best meal you've ever eaten.
Describe what you do on a hot day.	Compare a bicycle to a car.

Egg-straordinary Words

Random letters fall in painted sections of an egg carton when a player shakes it. The challenge is to create as many words as possible from those letters.

Age Range: 8 to 12
Skills Used: spelling, vocabulary knowledge
Number of Players: 2 to 6
Noise Level: moderate
Activity Level: low
Materials: egg carton, 36 disk-shaped tokens, pencil and paper, timer, paint

Setup

Paint four random sections of an egg carton any color. Write the alphabet on 26 tokens and then write another set of vowels and the letters *R, T, N, S,* and *L* on the extra 10 tokens.

How to Play

The first player puts all the tokens in the top of the egg carton, closes the lid, shakes the carton, and flips it over. No shaking is permitted after the flip is done. The cover is lifted, and disks that are in the painted sections of the carton are removed and shown to all the players to write on their papers. A timer is set, and each player writes as many words as possible using just those letters. Writing stops when the timer runs out, and each player draws a line across the paper at the end of his or her list.

Play continues in this way until each player has had a chance to shake the carton and pull out the letters. After the last player has had

a turn to shake the egg carton, players count the total number of words that they have on their sheets. Only correctly spelled words count in this game, and players are encouraged to check each other to catch misspellings so that the totals are accurate. The player with the most correct words wins.

Variations

■ For more advanced players, a few blank disks can be included in the set and used to represent any letter. More counters can also be added to the game to include consonant and vowel combinations.

■ Different point values can be assigned for words longer than three letters. For example, three-letter words count for one point, four-letter words for two points, five-letter words for three points, and six-letter (or more) words for four points.

Tips

■ If players work in teams for this game, mixing skill levels on the teams helps weaker players feel more successful and have more fun.

■ Have players check their words at the end of each round to make sure words are spelled correctly and that only the target letters have been used.

Flower Garden

Game pieces shaped like flowers in a garden are "picked" in turn, and players share words that start with the letter they find on the hidden end of the flower.

Age Range: 5 to 7

Skills Used: letter matching, phonetic awareness

Number of Players: 2 to 4

Noise Level: moderate

Activity Level: low

Materials: green craft sticks, silk flowers, 10" × 10" × 1" piece of green upholstery foam, permanent ink pen, cups

Setup

This game is played with game pieces fashioned like flowers and placed in slits cut in a foam "garden." Glue a silk flower head to the end of a green craft stick to create at least 26 game pieces. (If the flowers are all the same type and color, the game is more difficult but still appropriate for the age group.) Use a permanent ink pen to write a letter of the alphabet at the bottom of each flower's stick. The 10" × 10" × 1" foam piece should have enough slits cut in it to accommodate the number of flowers used. The slits can be cut in straight lines or randomly.

Before the game begins, the flowers are "planted" in the foam—with the letters hidden—to create a garden. Two flowers should be left out of the foam if either three or four players are playing the game. This is done to have an equal number of flowers available for picking to avoid giving an advantage to the two starting players.

How to Play

To play the game, each player selects a cup to serve as a vase. Players take turns "picking a flower" and reading the letter on it. To keep the flower, a player says a word that starts with the letter. If the answer is correct, the flower is put in his or her cup and play passes to the next player. If a player answers incorrectly or decides to pass, the flower is put back in any empty slot in the garden. The winner is the player with the most flowers after all the flowers have been chosen.

Variations

■ Additional flowers can be created for this game that show consonant combinations, such as *sh*. If this option is included, a *sh* word should not be accepted as an answer for picking the *s* flower.

■ Substitute uppercase and lowercase letters on the game pieces. Players try to find the matching pair of letters. So that this version of the game isn't too overwhelming, play with a small assortment of letters and either divide the garden in half or use only two types of flowers to differentiate uppercase and lowercase letters.

■ Use your garden for math by making pairs of flowers with a basic fact and an answer, dots and numbers, and so on.

■ Write pairs of synonyms, antonyms, or homonyms on the flower stems. Play in the same manner finding the flowers with words that go together.

Tip

■ An assortment of flowers can make this game appealing and serves as a memory aid for the youngest players.

Fractured Proverbs

This Concentration-style game allows players to match the beginnings and endings of well-known proverbs by turning over pairs of cards.

Age Range: 7 to 10
Skills Used: reading comprehension, proverb interpretation
Number of Players: 2
Noise Level: moderate
Activity Level: low
Materials: proverb cards

Setup

Cut apart and use the proverb cards provided or make your own by cutting 22 cards of the same size and color. Choose 11 familiar proverbs and write the first half of the proverb on one card and the second half on another.

How to Play

To play, place the cards facedown in rows and columns, Concentration-style. Players take turns flipping pairs of cards. If the pair includes the beginning and the end of the same proverb, the player explains its meaning and keeps the cards. When a match is made, the player gets another turn. If the cards do not match or the explanation of the proverb is wrong, play passes to the other player. When all the cards are matched, the player with the most cards is the winner.

Variation

■ This classic matching game can be modified for use in all sorts of content areas. For example, the matches could be states and their capitals, English and Spanish words, colors and color names, or rhyming words.

Tips

■ To speed up the game, matching cards can be written in a unique color of ink. This is a memory aid as well as a way to make the game self-checking.

■ Younger players can skip the explanation of the proverb.

Fractured Proverbs Cards

A stitch in time	saves nine.
Birds of a feather	flock together.
A penny saved	is a penny earned.
If the shoe fits,	wear it.
Strike while the iron	is hot.
Beware of Greeks	bearing gifts.
Beauty is	in the eye of the beholder.
Cross that bridge	when you come to it.
Pretty is	as pretty does.
Don't put all your eggs	in one basket.
Two is company,	three's a crowd.

Hopscotch Challenge

Players hop on certain spaces according to specified criteria on a challenge card.

Age Range: 5 to 10

Skills Used: gross motor skills, vocabulary knowledge

Number of Players: 3 to 4

Noise Level: moderate to high

Activity Level: high

Materials: challenge cards, chalk or tape to outline a hopscotch pattern

Setup

Draw a hopscotch pattern outside or on a nonskid rug or mat. Or, use tape to outline a hopscotch pattern on a tile floor or rug. Write various letters in spaces in the hopscotch.

Make challenge cards for players to draw to determine how they have to jump or what they have to do as they hop on the letters. Cards might read: Name the letters as you hop on them. Hop on the letters in sequence. Say a word that begins with the letter as you hop. Say a descriptive alliteration of three words starting with the letter (e.g., many mysterious monsters for *m* or friendly, freaky frogs for *f*).

How to Play

The first player draws a card and reads the challenge. He or she follows the directions on the card by hopping on one foot in the spaces in the hopscotch pattern. If the player meets the challenge, he or she scores a point. The card is returned to the deck, and the next player draws a card, reads the challenge, and follows the directions. Play continues in the same manner. After all of the players have had an equal number of turns, the scores are compared and the player with the most points wins.

Variations

- Rather than drawing a standard hopscotch, make a circular/snail-shaped hopscotch with home in the middle as shown in the hopscotch challenge patterns.

- Turn this into a challenge game among players by using a stopwatch to find the amount of time it takes to complete the directions. Record a player's time. Other players have the option to challenge and try to beat that time. If anyone can, that player earns a point. For each person who tries to beat the time but doesn't, the player who set the time earns a point.

- Use numbers rather than letters in the hopscotch. Challenge cards using numbers could be: Name the numbers as you hop on them. Hop on the numbers in sequence. Hop on numbers by 1s backward. Hop on numbers you'd use when counting by 2s. Hop on numbers you'd use when counting by 3s. Hop on all of the odd numbers. Hop on all of the even numbers. If the player hops in the proper spaces, a point is earned. The card is returned to the pack and the next player chooses a card and continues in the same manner.

Tips

Make hopping more interesting and challenging by having players do the following:

■ Kick a stone from space to space.

■ Carry a stone in an open palm.

■ Carry a stone on the back of their hand.

■ Bend over and carry a stone on their back.

■ Hop with another player, arms joined together.

Hopscotch Challenge Patterns

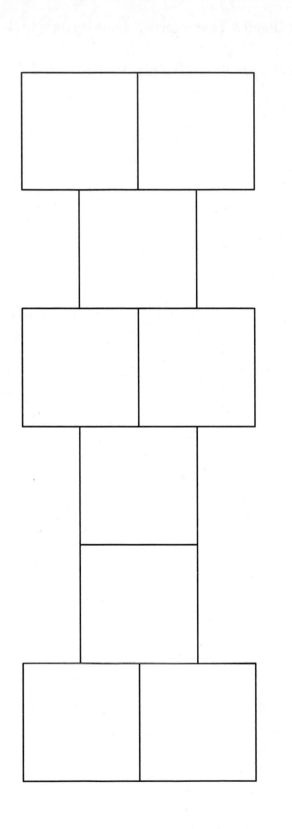

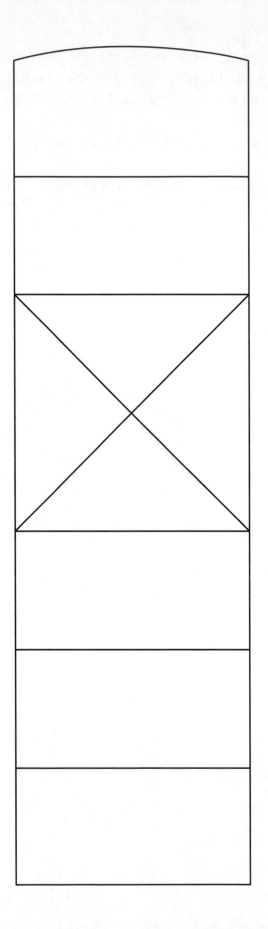

Hopscotch Challenge Patterns

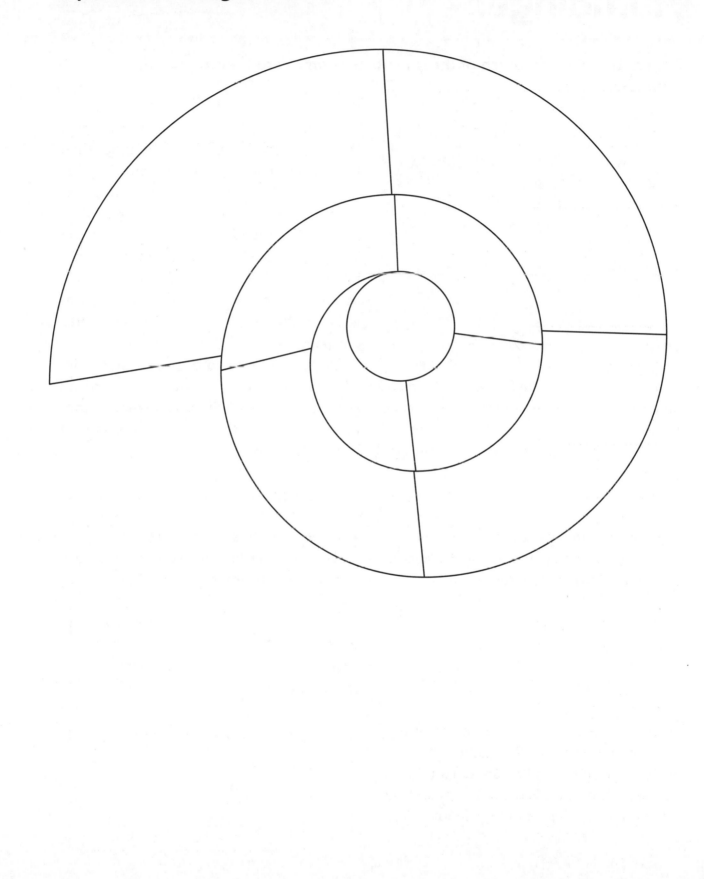

Humdinger

Players try to guess which of three sentences on a card their partner is humming.

Age Range: 8 to 12
Skills Used: listening, knowledge of syllabication, voice inflection
Number of Players: 4
Noise Level: moderate
Activity Level: low
Materials: game cards

Setup

Game cards are prepared with three simple, unrelated sentences or phrases on each card. There can be a mixture of questions, exclamations, and statements on a card, but they should be about the same length. For example, the following could be written on a card:

Come over to my house this weekend.
Where did you put my new pair of socks?
I decided to name my kitten Sandy.

A good play of this game would require about 40 cards.

How to Play

Players cooperate together in teams of two, sitting face-to-face, for this game. The starting team selects a card at random and turns it faceup. One player is the hummer and one is the guesser. The hummer silently selects one of the sentences or phrases and passes the card to the guesser. The hummer then hums the sentence without opening his or her lips. Gestures are allowed while the humming is done, but a team is disqualified if the gesture involves pointing to the card. The guesser can hear the hummed sentence up to three times if he or she requests, but then must guess which sentence on the card is being hummed. A correct guess scores one point.

Play passes to the other team and continues with the teams alternating and partners switching roles each time. The winning team has the most points when the cards have all been used.

Variations

■ A version of this game with players sitting back-to-back can be interesting because gestures are no longer possible.

■ If the guesser is wrong, another team can try to "steal" the point by guessing correctly. This variation only works if there are two teams playing the game.

Tips

. . . .

■ Players can contribute cards for this game once they are familiar with the way it is played.

■ Factual sentences can be used to reinforce specific content.

■ Sentences that summarize or retell a story can be used to reinforce the concept of beginning, middle, and end.

Ice Cream Colors

Players use a real ice cream scoop to get colored pom-poms out of a pail and match the color to the written words.

Age Range: 4 to 6

Skills Used: color knowledge, early reading

Number of Players: 2 to 4

Noise Level: moderate

Activity Level: low

Materials: ice cream scoop, 1.5- to 2-inch craft pom-poms in various colors, pail, game sheet, plastic spoons

Setup

Copy the sample game sheet and give one to each player along with a plastic spoon for fun. Fill the pail with at least two pom-poms of each color listed on the game sheet. One multicolored pom-pom should also be mixed into the pail.

How to Play

Players take turns dipping the ice cream scoop in the pail and removing a pom-pom without looking. The color word that matches the color of the pom-pom is crossed out on the game sheet and the pom-pom is put in the circle on the sheet, which represents a dish. The spoon is provided for pretend play between turns and at the end of the game. If the player draws a color that has already been added to the dish, it is returned to the pail and the turn passes to the next player.

The player drawing out the multicolored pom-pom becomes the instant winner of the game. If no one draws the instant win, then the player who is first to collect one pom-pom of each color wins the game.

Tips

■ To eliminate the problem of peeking at the colors during a turn, the player who scooped last can mix the pom-poms in the pail and hold it up a bit when the next player scoops.

■ Players should be allowed to continue to scoop until they get a pom-pom, rather than be penalized for having it fall out of the scoop on their turn.

■ For younger players who need more cues to read the color words, write the words in the corresponding colors to make the game easier.

■ Using real bowls can make the game more motivating for very young players.

Ice Cream Colors Game Sheet

yellow	green
blue	orange
red	purple
brown	pink
black	white

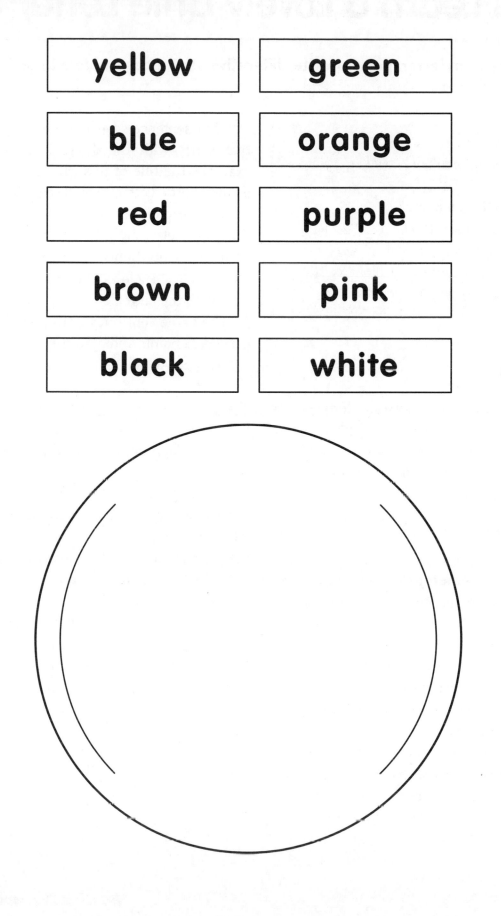

Let's Learn a Lovely Little Letter

Using a random letter, players write alliterative sentences within a time limit.

Age Range: 8 to 12

Skills Used: vocabulary knowledge, alliteration recognition

Number of Players: 2 to 5

Noise Level: moderate

Activity Level: low

Materials: letter and letter-blend cards, timer, scrap paper and pencils

Setup

Write alphabet letters and various letter blends (*th*, *wh*, *sh*, *ch*, etc.) on cards. Include five extra cards that have "Any letter" written on them. Shuffle and place the cards facedown in the center of the table.

How to Play

One player takes the top card and turns it over. The timer is set for three minutes, and each player writes down a sentence with words that start with the target letter. Scrap paper is available for jotting down ideas before the final answer is given. Once the time is up, players share their sentences relating to the letter.

Each sentence scores one point per word that starts with the designated letter. For example, the title of this game, "Let's Learn a Lovely Little Letter," would score five points. A maximum of four words not starting with the target letter are allowed in the sentence with no penalty. Subtract two points from the score for each additional word that doesn't start with the target letter.

The game continues until one player has earned 25 points and becomes the "Awesome Alliteration Achiever."

Tips

■ A list of approved connecting words can be provided on a card that is kept with the game deck. Sample connecting words can include *a*, *an*, *and*, *the*, and *of*. A longer list of permitted connecting words can be used to make the game easier and the penalty can be omitted from the scoring system.

■ The words must be spelled with the target letter rather than have the sound of the target letter. For example, *knife* is properly used for the target letter *k*, not *n*.

Link It

Teams of players try to make the longest chain of themed words linked by a common letter.

Age Range: 8 to 12
Skill Used: content vocabulary knowledge
Number of Players: 4 to 15
Noise Level: moderate to high
Activity Level: low to moderate
Materials: pencil and paper, timer

Setup

Choose a topic or category that has specific vocabulary. For example: food, plants, body parts.

How to Play

Teams of two or three players are formed. Each team has a piece of paper and a pencil. The game director announces the topic or theme for the game and sets the timer for five minutes. Starting with a word of their choice, each team tries to link as many related vocabulary words as possible. To link a word, a letter found in the previous word must be the initial letter in the next word. For example, for an Earth features theme the words might be ca*v*e, *v*olcano, *a*rch, *h*ill, *i*sthmus, *s*wamp, *m*ountain, and so on. An example for an animal theme would be shee*p*, *p*ig, *i*guana, *n*ewt, *w*hale, and so on.

When time is up, each team shares their chain with the other teams. If the linking rule was followed, they score one point for each word. The team with the most points or linked words is the winner.

Variation

■ Have the whole group brainstorm a list of words to use for a cooperative version of this game. Divide the list equally among the players. Give each player that number of chain link or puzzle piece outlines as shown. The players cut out and copy their assigned theme words on each. When everyone is done cutting and writing, the player selected to go first puts a word out on the floor. The next player tries to add to the chain following the rules previously described and so on. Players can pass if they don't have a word that will link. The game stops when no one has a word to link or someone runs out of words.

Tips

■ Record how long the players made the chain. Let players try to beat the record on their own.

■ Play the game for more than one day. Allow players to research words in order to continue the chain. Provide time each day for them to add to their chain.

Link It Puzzle Piece and Chain Link Patterns

(Use for the cooperative version.)

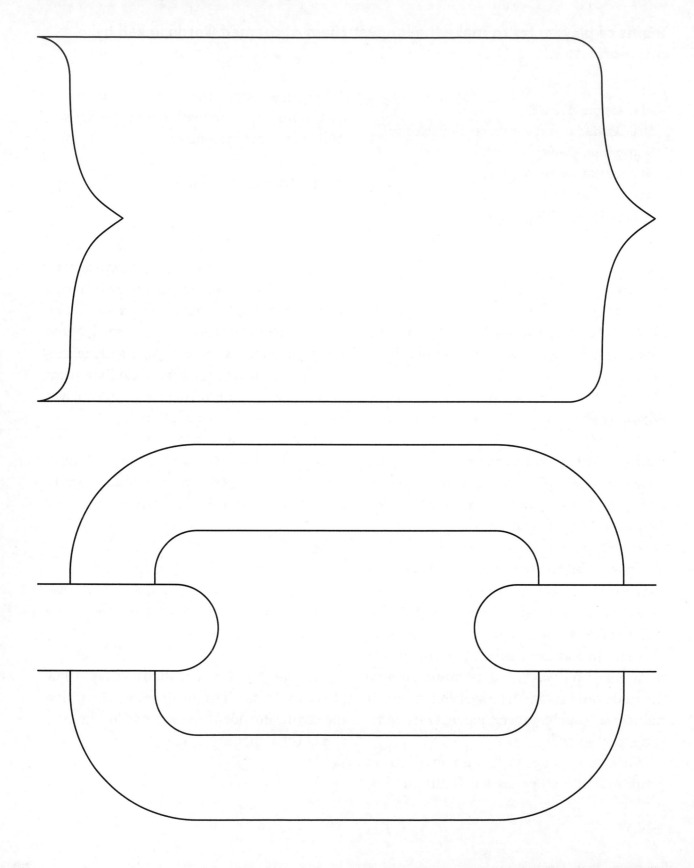

The Odd One Wins!

Players read sets of sentences to locate the one that isn't "on topic."

Age Range: 7 to 10
Skill Used: identifying sentences on topic
Number of Players: 4
Noise Level: low
Activity Level: low
Materials: sets of topic sentence cards
(four cards/set)

Setup

Create several packs of four cards each. Write one sentence on each of the cards. Three of the sentences should be about the same topic. One sentence is off topic. For example: Dogs like to play. Collars and leashes are needed for dogs. Dogs come in different sizes. People live in houses.

How to Play

The players select a pack of four cards. One card is dealt to each player. Each player reads his or her card to the others. The player whose card is off topic announces this to the other players. If everyone agrees, the player with that card gets all of the other cards. Deal out the next set of cards. The game ends when all of the card sets have been used. The winner is the player with the most cards.

Variation

■ For each set of four cards, write three equations that equal the same answer and one with a different answer.

Tips

■ Use a different color paper or cardstock for each set of cards to easily sort them in preparation for the next game.

■ Have students make lists of sentences related to their interests. Use these lists to create the sets of cards.

On the Hunt

Players hunt for words hidden in a grid.

Age Range: 6 to 12

Skills Used: vocabulary knowledge, spelling

Number of Players: 2 to 24

Noise Level: low

Activity Level: low

Materials: graph paper, list of vocabulary words, timer

Setup

Give each player the vocabulary list and a sheet of graph paper. Be sure enough time is given for the students to create the word hunts.

How to Play

Players write the selected words in various places horizontally, vertically, and diagonally on the graph paper by putting each letter of the word in neighboring boxes. Encourage the players to connect the words by using common letters. When all of the words are written on the paper, the player fills in the remaining spaces with other letters. When all of the players are done, papers are exchanged. Set a timer. Players hunt for the words and circle them when found. When time runs out, the words found are counted. The player who found the most is the winner.

Tips

■ Be sure students are familiar with doing word searches.

■ Demonstrate how to use common letters to link words vertically and horizontally.

■ For a quick way to fill in the empty spaces, just write the alphabet.

■ Make a copy of the word placements prior to the student filling in the empty spaces. This copy can be used for clues for locations of words that are difficult to find.

■ Use graph paper with fewer and larger spaces for younger students.

■ If enough words have not been located, play it again. Have the players use a different color pencil or marker to make counting words found on the second round easier.

Pass a Laugh

Working together, players construct amusing sentences by adding a word at a time on a paper going around the circle.

Age Range: 8 to 12

Skill Used: sentence construction

Number of Players: 8

Noise Level: moderate

Activity Level: low

Materials: pencil and paper

Setup

None needed.

How to Play

All of the players sit in a circle with their own paper and pencil. The game starts by each player writing a word in the middle of their paper. Everyone passes his or her paper to the player to the left. That player reads the word and adds another word in an attempt to make a sentence. Continue in this manner for a certain number of passes or until the papers go all the way around the circle.

Players can use an editing mark to add a word between others. Players can also add a prefix or suffix to a word. Read the sentences at the end and have the players vote for the funniest sentence.

Tip

■ Cut self-stick notes into strips so the adhesive portion is on one end. Then instead of writing words on the blank paper, players can write their words on the self-stick note and stick it to the paper.

Picture This

Players cooperate to tell a story relating to randomly chosen pictures.

Age Range: 9 to 12
Skills Used: storytelling, creativity
Number of Players: 4 to 6
Noise Level: moderate
Activity Level: low
Materials: magazine pictures, cloth bag, game sheet, erasable marker, pair of dice

Setup

The magazine pictures for this game should be in color and show items of interest to the players, such as cars, animals, and people playing sports. There can also be pictures of scenery, indoor spaces, and objects such as boats, toys, dishes, lawn mowers, and camping tents. Pictures of fantasy creatures, including unicorns and leprechauns, will also add a bit of whimsy to playing this game. The pictures should be at least 3″ × 5″, and it is best if they are laminated or mounted on cardstock before being mixed into a cloth bag. A minimum of 12 pictures should be prepared.

Copy and use the game sheet of story elements provided or make your own. This game sheet is needed as a reference during the game. It can be reused if it has been laminated and is then marked using an erasable marker; it is wiped clean after each story.

How to Play

Players sit in a circle and pass the game sheet around. Each person in the group rolls the dice and marks the story element corresponding to the value of the roll. If a player rolls a number that is already marked, he or she continues rolling until another story element can be selected. Once marked, the sheet is placed where all players can see it. The first player takes a picture from the bag without looking and begins a story relating to something in it. If any of the checked items on the sheet are included in that part of the story, players score a point for the group. Any player can identify the use of a story element and record its use on the story card by crossing through the check mark. Elements included in the story, but not checked, do not need to be recorded.

When the first player completes a portion of the story, the bag of pictures is passed to the next person who also draws a picture. The bag can be passed whether or not a checked story element has been identified, and the turn can be of any length, but should not be a complete story.

The players continue the game by adding to the story based upon the picture they draw while everyone listens for story elements. If the bag returns to the player who began the story, the game can continue, but no new pictures are drawn from the bag. The game continues until all the marked story elements have been included and identified in the group's story.

Variation

■ Teams can score two points for a checked element and one point for any additional item included after a set number of turns. This allows teams to compete against each other to develop interesting and complex stories.

Tip

■ Players can contribute photos for this game to make the stories more personal and interesting.

Picture This Game Sheet

✔	Roll	Element
	2	Adding a character
	3	Telling how the character changes
	4	Describing the setting
	5	Inventing a problem to be solved
	6	Solving a problem
	7	Adding humor
	8	Including an unexpected element
	9	Having a happy ending
	10	Giving the story a title
	11	Adding a fantasy element
	12	Adding a sad element

Popular Picks

Players strategically choose words from a textbook passage in an effort to match the words also chosen by other players. Points are scored for the most popular picks.

Age Range: 6 to 12

Skills Used: key word recognition, strategic thinking

Number of Players: 8 to 24

Noise Level: moderate to high

Activity Level: moderate

Materials: a common textbook, handout, or written list; self-stick notes; pencil or marker

Setup

Distribute five self-stick notes to each player. Have enough space on the board or a wall for players to stick these notes.

How to Play

Each player writes his or her initials on a corner of the five self-stick notes. The players all read a common text selection (science and social studies materials work well for this game). From that text, each player chooses five important words and writes one on each self-stick note. Players put a star on one word they have chosen that they think most of the other players will also choose.

When everyone has finished reading and writing, players take turns putting their notes on the board or a wall, in graph fashion, matching their words to others that might have already been placed there. Players agree on the word written on the most self-stick notes. Everyone who chose that word is a winner. Players who have a star on that word note become Super Winners.

Tips

■ Have the Super Winners share why they chose and starred a particular word.

■ Use the data to generate graphs, story problems, greater than/less than sentences, percentages, and range, mean, median, or mode.

Progressive Pictures

Players pass papers around the group, adding lines to each other's work. The resulting picture is described and given a title when shared at the end.

Age Range: 5 and up

Skills Used: creativity, verbal expression

Number of Players: 6 to 10

Noise Level: low

Activity Level: low

Materials: blank drawing paper and markers of various colors for each player, timer

Setup

None needed.

How to Play

Players need to have a drawing surface available and be seated in a circle within easy reach of each other. Each player begins the game with a blank sheet of paper and a different color marker to use for the whole game.

When the game director sets the timer for one minute and gives a signal, each player begins drawing on his or her paper, using one continuous line. The drawing can be an abstract shape, a recognizable polygon, or a recognizable object, but the marker must always remain in contact with the paper. There are no limits on how long the line must be or whether or not it can cross itself.

At the end of the time, players pass their papers to the next person in order. The players then add a line to the existing drawing without lifting their marker. This continues until each player has added to every picture.

Players take turns showing the completed pictures, giving each one a title, and telling what they see in each picture. Other players can add their observations and explain what they had in mind when they put their mark on the picture.

Variations

■ Put limitations on the drawings to change the types of pictures created. For example, players might be required to leave at least one end of a line showing when they pass the paper. The next player would then have to start drawing from that point. Or, a rule could be made that no line can cross another line.

■ For a more complicated game, the group might try interpreting different types of music in their drawing to see how the drawings reflect the background sounds.

■ Players can write about the pictures when complete. Make a book of all the pictures and stories or mount the stories with the pictures and put them on display.

Tips

■ Demonstrate this game on a board or large sheet of paper while everyone watches the development of the picture. When finished, players can take turns telling what they see in the picture and discussing the ways different lines influenced the final drawing. This can prepare players for the paper passing game.

■ This game is naturally quiet, so it might be helpful to calm a group down before playing it. Calming music in the background can help to establish a good atmosphere for "Progressive Pictures."

Quintessential Game

Players brainstorm and compare examples of a category to decide which one is "quintessential."

Age Range: 9 to 12
Skills Used: reasoning, persuasion, factual knowledge
Number of Players: 3 to 10
Noise Level: moderate
Activity Level: low
Materials: question cards, whiteboards, markers

Setup

Question cards are prepared for this game. The questions are in this format:

"What is the quintessential _____ of _____?" *or*

"Who is the quintessential _____ of _____?"

How to Play

Divide players into three or more teams to play the game. Each team has a whiteboard and markers to use for recording answers. Question cards are placed facedown on the table and drawn one at a time. Anyone can read the question, and then each team quietly discusses their response and writes it on their board. When all groups are ready, the responses are revealed simultaneously and discussed together. Consensus is reached regarding the best answer and teams with that response get a point. *Quintessential* is understood to be the most representative and definitive example of something, and this criterion is used to reach consensus regarding the best answer.

Choosing the best answer is usually fairly obvious, but occasionally it may be difficult. For example, suppose the question is "What is the quintessential mountain in the world?" An argument could be made for Everest as the best answer, but a team with the answer Krakatoa might be able to persuade the group to agree that the powerful eruption of Krakatoa made it more important, influential, and quintessential than Everest. The actual decision about the answer is less important than the process of reaching it. A serious controversy can be solved by awarding no points at all and moving on.

Tips

■ Playing this game in transitional settings such as bus rides, walks, and waiting in line is fun. Anyone can propose a question, and anyone can answer and stimulate discussion.

■ Make a special Quintessential Box where students can place questions they've created for this game. Use these when the time is appropriate.

Quintessential Game

What is the quintessential product of Wisconsin?	What is the quintessential sport of the Winter Olympics?	Who is the quintessential writer in history?	What is the quintessential ancient civilization in the world?	What is the quintessential game in history?
What is the quintessential mammal of Hawaii?	Who is the quintessential president of the United States?	What is the quintessential building in the world?	What is the quintessential pet in the world?	Who is the quintessential pirate in history?
What is the quintessential mountain in the world?	What is the quintessential battle of the Civil War?	What is the quintessential city in the United States?	What is the quintessential sport in the United States?	What is the quintessential river in the world?

What is the quintessential song in the United States?	What is the quintessential endangered species in the world?	What is the quintessential extinct animal in the world?
Who is the quintessential criminal in history?	Who is the quintessential ruler in history?	What is the quintessential dance of Ireland?
What is the quintessential book in —— grade?	Who is the quintessential artist in history?	Who is the quintessential children's author in the United States?
What is the quintessential planet in the universe?	What is the quintessential element in the atmosphere?	What is the quintessential thing a baby needs?

Rainbow

Players draw word cards with color names on them and color in their blank rainbow sheets.

Age Range: 4 to 6

Skills Used: early reading, fine motor skill, color knowledge

Number of Players: 2 to 4

Noise Level: low

Activity Level: low

Materials: rainbow sheet, crayons, cloth bag, cards with color names on them

Setup

Use the black-and-white drawing of a rainbow with the color names written in the spaces as provided, making copies for each player. The rainbow recommended for this game is a six-color drawing omitting the "indigo" section that appears in more scientific diagrams. The game also requires six reusable cards with the color names written on them. Make your own color word cards or copy and cut out the cards supplied. Cards are placed in a cloth bag.

How to Play

Each player is given a rainbow sheet. The first player draws a color card from the bag, reads it, and colors the matching area on his or her rainbow. The card is returned to the bag, and players continue to take turns picking a card and coloring their rainbows. If a player selects a color card for a space already colored on his or her rainbow, the card is returned to the bag and play passes to the next player. The first one to completely color the rainbow is the winner. The rest of the players can continue until everyone has colored the whole rainbow.

Variation

■ One or two "Any Color" cards can be included in the bag. This is a "wild" card. A player who picks this card may color any remaining section of his or her rainbow.

Tips

■ Make the game easier by writing the names of the color words in the appropriate color. "Any Color" can be written with each letter in a different color.

■ "Purple" can be substituted for "Violet" if desired.

■ Try leaving the names of the colors off of the rainbow sheets and provide a model for players to copy.

Rainbow Color Cards

red	yellow
blue	green
violet	orange
any color	any color

Rainbow Sheet

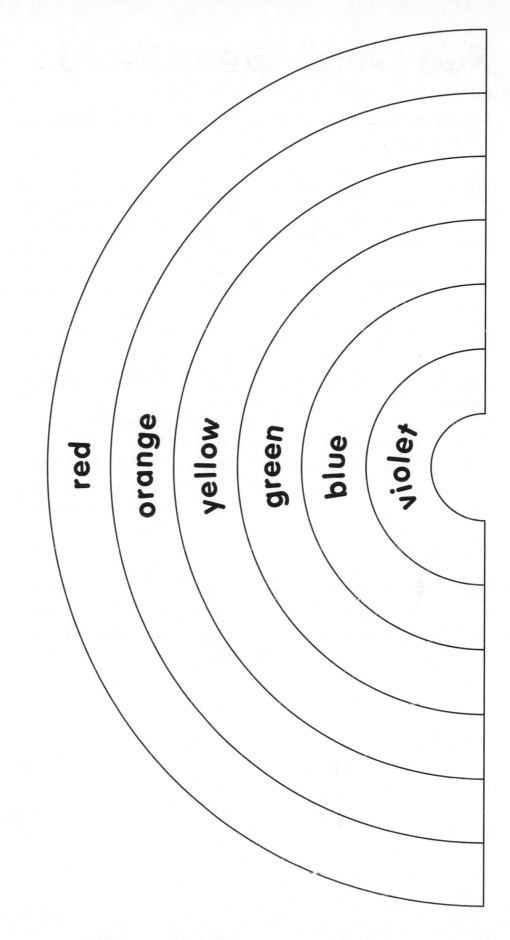

Red Word, Green Word

Players read word cards but only win them if they can read the special words written in red.

> **Age Range:** 6 to 10
> **Skill Used:** reading
> **Number of Players:** 2 to 4
> **Noise Level:** low to moderate
> **Activity Level:** low
> **Materials:** vocabulary cards, red marker, green marker

Setup

Create a large pack of vocabulary cards appropriate for players' ages and/or reading levels. Write most of the words in green and several in red.

How to Play

Place all of the vocabulary cards facedown in a pile between the players. The first person draws a card off the top of the pile. If the card is green and the player can read the word, the player holds the word card and draws again. If the player can't read the green word, it is told to him or her. The player repeats the word and places the card on the bottom of the pile. It becomes the next player's turn.

Players continue drawing cards and reading words until a red card is turned up. If the player can read the red card, that player keeps all of the cards he or she has read and it becomes the next player's turn. If the red word can't be read correctly, all of the cards that player has read on that turn are placed at the bottom of the pile. The game ends when there are no more cards to read. The winner is the player with the most cards.

Variation

■ Make packs with math facts or equations written in red and green. Players tell the answers to continue drawing or to keep their cards.

Tips

■ Tricky words or new vocabulary words are great choices for red words.

■ Words to emphasize or that need extra practice can occur several times in the pack.

Scratch My Back

The player with the alphabet sheet on his or her back is the "scratcher" and points to various letters with a backscratcher. The rest of the players compete to make a word from the letters being "scratched."

Age Range: 5 to 9
Skills Used: vocabulary knowledge, spelling
Number of Players: 3 to 5
Noise Level: moderate
Activity Level: low
Materials: backscratcher, game board, paper, pencil, string

Setup

This game requires a game board—a piece of paper with the alphabet scattered upon it. The game board shown can be copied or create your own. If you make your own board, each letter (uppercase and lowercase written together) should occupy a separate space on the sheet in a random pattern. Common letters, such as *R, T, N, S, L,* and the vowels, should be in larger areas, while uncommon letters, such as *V, X, Z, J,* and *Q,* should appear in smaller areas. No area should be smaller than the end of the backscratcher. Once prepared, this game board should be laminated and punched with two holes. Attach string so that the board can hang around the player's neck. Players must have their own paper and pencil.

How to Play

One player is designated the "scratcher" and puts the game board on his or her back. The other players sit where they can all see the sheet. Then the scratcher says, "I have an itch" and begins to move the end of the backscratcher around on the card, bringing it to a stop and saying, "Right there!" The end of the backscratcher should be pointing to a particular letter, but if it falls on a line, players can ask for the scratch to be a little higher, lower, to the left, or to the right. Players write the letter on their papers and ask for another scratch.

Letters continue to be "scratched" until one of the players is able to make a word with the selected letters. The first one to write a correctly spelled word wins the round and trades places with the scratcher. Play begins again.

Players can decide on a minimum length for winning words before they begin the game so that extremely short words do not score. Three-letter words might be a reasonable minimum length allowed for a play of this game.

Variations

■ Have younger players call out a word starting with the letter that is scratched. The first player to get five correct words would then take the place of the scratcher.

■ Change some of the letters to consonant clusters (*th*, *sh*, *ch*, *wh*, and so on), prefixes, or suffixes to use a particular language skill.

Tip

. . . .

■ Some players might need a judge available to determine if their words are spelled correctly or if their words actually start with the target letters. An adult volunteer or older "buddy" could serve in this role to make the game run more smoothly.

Scratch My Back Game Board

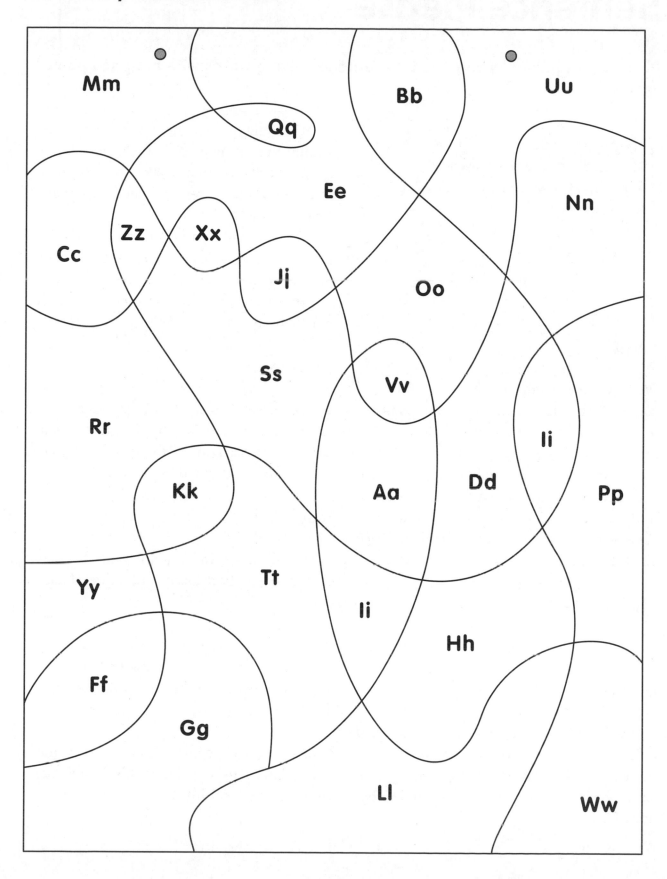

Sentence Please

Players earn points by constructing sentences using words with assigned point values.

Age Range: 8 to 11
Skill Used: sentence construction
Number of Players: 2 to 6
Noise Level: low
Activity Level: low
Materials: word cards, cloth bag, two-minute timer

Setup

Write various words on paper of different colors. Each color has its own point value; it is written on the card as well. For instance, green could equal one point, orange could equal two points, and so on. Be sure to include several words from each part of speech. Make multiple cards of words commonly used in sentences such as *the, a, and, is,* and *are.* Place all of the cards in a cloth bag.

How to Play

Each player draws eight word cards from the cloth bag and places them faceup. The timer is set for two minutes. During the time, each player tries to construct a sentence using as many of his or her words as possible. If a player is unable to make a sentence, as in the case of drawing no verb, he or she can exchange the highest value card for another draw from the bag.

At the end of the time, players take turns reading their sentences. If the other players agree that the sentence makes sense, points for each word card used are added up to make the player's score.

To start the next round, all of the used word cards are thrown back into the bag and mixed and each player draws eight cards again. The person with the most points after five rounds is the winner.

Variation

■ Use different color cards to designate various parts of speech. Each part of speech could be worth an assigned point value or a point value could be assigned to each word.

Tips

■ Instead of writing a point value on each card, make a chart listing the value of each color.

■ To use this game to prepare students for a vocabulary quiz, write those important vocabulary words on the color with the highest point value.

■ To add an element of luck to the game, write a few high-frequency words on the color with the highest point value.

Shoebox

Teams take turns making compound words that start with a smaller word drawn from a box of cards.

Age Range: 8 to 11
Skills Used: vocabulary knowledge, reading
Number of Players: 2 to 6
Noise Level: moderate
Activity Level: low
Materials: shoebox, word cards

Setup

Create word cards using words that form the beginning half of common compound words, or use the sample cards provided. Cards are prepared, shuffled, and put in the box before the game is played.

How to Play

Players divide into two teams and put the shoebox within easy reach. The first team pulls a card from the box and thinks of a compound word containing the word selected. For example, if they selected *butter*, the team might say, "Scotch." The other team would then attempt to think of another compound word for *butter*, such as *butterfly*.

The two teams take turns thinking of compound words using the target word until one team can't think of an answer. The last team to give an answer keeps the card. Teams take turns drawing cards and thinking of words. The first team to collect 10 cards wins.

As a starting point, possible answers follow for each of the words provided on the sample card sheet. Other examples are easily gathered from a dictionary.

air—airbags, aircraft, airfield, airmail, airplane, airport, airtight, airtime
any—anybody, anyhow, anymore, anyplace, anything, anytime, anyway, anywhere
back—backache, backbiting, backboard, backbone, backbreaking, backdrop, backfire, background, backhand, backlash, backlog, backpack, backrest, backrub, backspace, backspin, backstab, backstop, backstretch, backstroke, backtrack, backup, backwater, backwoods
bath—bathhouse, bathrobe, bathroom, bathtub
bed—bedclothes, bedpost, bedridden, bedrock, bedroll, bedroom, bedside, bedspread, bedtime
black—blackbird, blackboard, blacklist, blackmail, blacksmith, blacktop
blue—blueberry, bluebeard, bluebell, bluebird, blueblood, bluegrass, bluenose
book—bookcase, bookkeeper, bookman, bookmark, bookshelf, bookstore, bookworm
butter—butterball, buttercup, butterfat, butterfingers, butterfly, buttermilk, butternut, butterscotch
camp—campfire, campground, campout, campsite, campstool

cow—cowbell, cowboy, cowpoke

day—daybook, daybreak, daycare, daydream, daylight, daytime

door—doorbell, doorknob, doorman, doormat, doorstep, doorstop

down—downbeat, downcast, downfall, downgrade, downhill, download, downplay, downpour, downside, downspout, downstairs, downstream, downturn

ear—earache, earmark, earmuff, earphone, earring, earwax

every—everybody, everyday, everyone, everything, everywhere

eye—eyeball, eyebrow, eyeglass, eyelash, eyelid, eyesight, eyesore, eyewitness

fire—firearm, firecracker, firefighter, firefly, fireman, fireplace, fireproof, fireworks

foot—football, footlights, footloose, footman, footnote, footprint, footrest, footstep, footstool, footwork

grand—granddaddy, grandfather, grandma, grandmamma, grandmother, grandpa, grandstand

hand—handbag, handball, handbook, handcuff, handwriting

head—headache, headdress, headhunt, headlight, headlong, headmaster, headmistress, headquarters, headstone, headstrong, headway

heart—heartache, heartbreak, heartfelt, heartsick, heartstrings, heartwarming

high—highbrow, highchair, highlight, highroad, highway

home—homebody, homeboy, homecoming, homegrown, homemade, homeroom, homesick, homespun, hometown, homework

in—income, indoor, infield, inland, inlet, input, inside, instep, into

land—landfall, landfill, landlord, landmark, landowner, landscape, landslide

life—lifeboat, lifeguard, lifelike, lifeline, lifelong, lifesaver, lifestyle, lifetime, lifework

mail—mailbox, mailman, mailroom

night—nightclub, nightfall, nightgown, nightlight, nightmare, nightshade, nightstand, nighttime

out—outburst, outcast, outclass, outcome, outcry, outdo, outdoors, outfield, outfit, outgoing, outgrow, outhouse, outlaw, outlet, outlook, outnumber, outpatient, output, outside, outskirts, outstretched

over—overall, overbearing, overboard, overcoat, overcome, overdo, overdose, overdue, overflow, overfull, overhang, overhaul, overhead, overland, overlap, overload, overlook, overpaid, overpower, overseas, oversee, overseer, overshadow, overshoes, oversized, oversleep, overstate, overtake, overtime, overturn, overuse, overvalue, overweight, overwork

play—playground, playmate, playpen, playroom, plaything, playtime

post—postdate, postfix, postmark, postman, postmaster

sand—sandbag, sandbox, sandpaper, sandstone

sea—seaside, seafood, seaman, seaport, seashell, seashore, seaway, seaweed

short—shortchange, shortcoming, shortcut, shortfall, shortstop

snow—snowball, snowblower, snowboard, snowflake, snowman, snowmobile, snowplow, snowscape, snowstorm

some—somebody, someday, somehow, someone, someplace, something, sometime, somewhat, somewhere

sun—sunburn, sunflower, sunlight, sunshade, suntan

super—superhero, superhuman, superimpose, supermarket, supernatural, supersize

under—underclothing, undercook, undercover, undercurrent, underdog, undergo, underground, undergrowth, underhand, underline, undermined, underside, undersized, understatement, undertaker, undervalued, underwear, underweight

up—upbeat, update, upgrade, uphill, upkeep, uplift, upon, upright, uproot, upstage, upstairs, uptake

water—watercolor, waterfall, waterlogged, watermelon, waterproof, waterscape

wood—woodcutter, woodland, woodpile, woodpecker, woodshed, woodwork, woodworm

Variation

■ This game is meant to include only actual compound words such as *bedbug*, not common pairs of words or open compounds as in *bed rest*. However, for younger players, common pairs might be accepted to move the game along and improve vocabulary skills.

Tips

■ Use an online dictionary to settle disputes so players can't get ideas from the surrounding words as can happen with a printed dictionary. If the challenging team is correct, they earn the card. If they are not correct, the other team earns the card and another turn.

■ Brainstorm closed compound words using common word parts. Use those combinations to make up the cards for this game.

Shoebox Cards

bed	camp	ear	grand	home
bath	butter	down	foot	high
back	book	door	fire	heart
any	blue	day	eye	head
air	black	cow	every	hand

Shoebox Cards (continued)

night	mail	life	land	in
sand	post	play	over	out
sun	some	snow	short	sea
wood	water	up	under	super

Shop 'Til You Drop

Players fill their shopping bags with cards having the same initial sound.

Age Range: 6 to 8

Skill Used: recognition of initial consonant sounds

Number of Players: 4 to 6

Noise Level: moderate

Activity Level: low

Materials: shopping cards, a "shopping" bag for each player

Setup

Prepare shopping cards by cutting out pictures from catalogs or writing words that correspond with items you can find at certain types of stores. For grocery cards, for example, words or pictures can be cut from food labels.

How to Play

Each player chooses some sort of bag (lunch bag, little gift bag with handles, and so on). All of the shopping cards are dealt into the players' bags. Taking turns, a player randomly draws a card out of his or her shopping bag. The player looks at the card and asks for cards that begin with the initial letter of that item. For example the player draws a card with a picture of a carton of milk. That person would ask, "Who bought something that starts like *milk*?" All of the players would look for items in their shopping bags that start with *m*. One might answer, "I have *mittens* and *markers*." Another could answer, "I have *marshmallows*." Another could answer, "I have nothing that starts like *milk*."

Players with cards that match the requested sound hand those cards to the first player, who puts them in a pile. Play continues until someone runs out of cards in his or her bag. The winner is the player who has the most cards.

Tip

■ The skill level of this game changes if just words are written on the cards or if pictures with no word clues are used.

Superlative Scavenger Hunt

Teams explore an outdoor area to find and collect items that fit descriptive categories.

Age Range: 7 to 12
Skill Used: knowledge of adjectives
Number of Players: 6 to 24
Noise Level: moderate
Activity Level: high
Materials: adjective card, paper bags

Setup

A list of 8 to 10 adjectives should be written on a card and duplicated for each team participating in the game. Suggested words are shown on the sample card. These lists can be stapled, glued, or taped to the paper bags.

How to Play

Pairs of players explore a designated outdoor natural area to gather objects that display each of the listed characteristics (for example, *fragrant*, *prickly*, *perforated*, and so on). The teams reconvene after a designated time limit to show their collections and explain their choices. Players vote for the best example of each description, and the pair with the most votes for their item wins a point. The pair with the most points overall, wins the game.

Variation

■ This can be played as an indoor game. For this version of the hunt, pairs simply write down their choices on the list of adjectives, rather than actually collect them, so bags are not needed.

■ Customize the terms to a field trip site to encourage players to be observant. For example, a trip to a historic site could include such terms as *antiquated*, *clever*, *unexpected*, and *patriotic*. The items cannot be collected in this version but can be listed.

Tips

■ Make the list of adjectives age-appropriate. Harder words might include *delicate*, *variegated*, and *substantial*. Beginner words might include *hard*, *soft*, and *pretty*.

■ When gathering items outside, be sure the players show respect for the environment by following basic collection rules such as never picking the last flower in an area, not pulling bark off of a tree, not collecting animals, being gentle, and so on.

■ Pair verbal players with less verbal players to make the sharing part of the game go more smoothly.

Superlative Scavenger Hunt Card

Superlative Scavenger Hunt Card

1. fragrant _____
2. prickly _____
3. perforate _____
4. smooth _____
5. rough _____
6. colorful _____
7. sticky _____
8. flat _____
9. fragile _____
10. _____

Superlative Scavenger Hunt Card

1. fragrant _____
2. prickly _____
3. perforate _____
4. smooth _____
5. rough _____
6. colorful _____
7. sticky _____
8. flat _____
9. fragile _____
10. _____

Superlative Scavenger Hunt Card

1. fragrant _____
2. prickly _____
3. perforate _____
4. smooth _____
5. rough _____
6. colorful _____
7. sticky _____
8. flat _____
9. fragile _____
10. _____

Superlative Scavenger Hunt Card

1. fragrant _____
2. prickly _____
3. perforate _____
4. smooth _____
5. rough _____
6. colorful _____
7. sticky _____
8. flat _____
9. fragile _____
10. _____

Switcho Change-O

Players construct a new type of sentence by building on the initial letter of each word.

Age Range: 8 to 12
Skills Used: vocabulary knowledge, recognition of sentence types
Number of Players: 2 to 8
Noise Level: moderate
Activity Level: low
Materials: marker board or chart paper, markers, pencil and paper, upholstery foam die

Setup

Make a die out of the upholstery foam. On each side write *funny, serious, command, question, statement,* and *free choice.*

How to Play

Have each player write a sentence. The first player reads his or her sentence out loud and copies it onto the board or chart paper so all players can see it. The player hands the die to another player who rolls it and announces the word that turns up. Everyone says, "Switcho change-o!" Everyone, except the first player, creates a new sentence by using the first letter of each word. For example, for a funny or free choice sentence, *Cats like to drink milk* could change to *Cousin Luke tagged dangerous monsters.*

As players complete their new sentences, they say, "Switcho change-o!" Players read their sentences and vote to allow the ones that match the roll of the die. Those that match, earn a point. Play several rounds. The player with the most points wins.

Variations

■ Use sentences from a textbook.

■ Create new sentences using the ending letter of each word.

Tips

■ Keep a box available for students to put favorite sentences in. On game day, draw a sentence from the box. The person who submitted that sentence gets to direct the game.

■ Set a timer for writing time (20 to 30 seconds per word is a good amount of time).

Twinkle, Twinkle

Players construct star puzzles using knowledge of rhyming words.

Age Range: 5 to 8
Skill Used: rhyming
Number of Players: 2 to 4
Noise Level: low
Activity Level: low
Materials: tagboard, star template

Setup

Create star puzzles from the tagboard using the template shown. Each star will have a center piece and five arms. Then write a rhyming word in the middle of each star and five additional rhyming words on each arm of the star. For example, in the center write *star* and on each arm write *car, far, tar, are,* or *scar.* Cut the pieces apart.

How to Play

Deal the centers of the stars out to the players so all have an equal number. Players take turns turning the stars' centers up and reading the word found in the center of each star. Place the star points, facedown, in the center between the players. Players take turns choosing a point and reading the word on it. If the word rhymes with one of the player's star centers, the point is placed on that star. Play continues until someone adds five points to his or her star and becomes the winner.

Variations

■ Write a number in the center of the star. On the points write problems that equal that number. For example, in the center write 10. On each arm write in the problems: $1 + 9$, $2 + 8$, $5 + 5$, $12 - 2$, $15 - 5$.

■ Write an animal group in the center of the star. On the points, write the names of animals that belong to that group. For example in the center write *bird.* On each arm add *eagle, robin, owl, penguin,* and *ostrich.* For this game, the center section can be repeated but don't duplicate the words on the arms of the stars.

Tip

■ To help students just beginning to learn rhyming especially when alternate letter patterns are used, put a unique symbol on the star center and the matching points.

Twinkle, Twinkle Pattern

(Makes two stars.)

Who, What, When, Where, Why, and How?

Papers are passed and players add parts to a story without knowing what has already been written.

Age Range: 8 to 12
Skill Used: creative writing
Number of Players: 3 to 6
Noise Level: moderate
Activity Level: low
Materials: game sheet for each player, pencils, paper clips

Setup

Copy the game sheet provided or create your own. The game sheet is divided from top to bottom in seven sections. The top section is blank. The remaining sections have *who, what, when, where, why,* and *how* written in them. Each player needs a game sheet.

How to Play

The game begins with all players writing a response in the "who" section of their sheet. Players make up any character they wish and write at least one sentence describing the character in this section of the game sheet. There is no need for players to invent characters that relate to each other because each sheet will become a complete story in itself. When everyone is finished with the "who" space, the blank section at the top of the paper is folded down over the writing and held with a paper clip. Papers are passed in a circle to the next person on the left. Without reading what is already on the sheet, players then write a sentence or two about what happens to the character in the story. This section is folded over and clipped to hide the writing before the paper is again passed to the left.

Play continues with each person writing in the next available spot to create a complete story on each paper. When the last section is filled in on each sheet, the paper is passed one more time. Players open the sheets and read the resulting stories to the group.

Variations

■ The words on the game sheet can be changed to *character, setting, conflict, rising action, climax,* and *resolution.*

■ Recycle the responses into new stories by cutting the sections apart and putting them in separate piles or containers. Players will draw one slip from each pile and create a new story.

Tip

■ Let the players decide if a timer should be used for this game. They know if the game needs to be moved along or if timing would add too much pressure.

Who, What, When, Where, Why, and How? Game Sheet

Fold

Who

Fold

What

Fold

When

Fold

Where

Fold

Why

Fold

How

X Word

Players use a tic-tac-toe board to strategically fill in letters to make words.

Age Range: 7 to 12

Skills Used: vocabulary knowledge, spelling, strategic thinking

Number of Players: 2

Noise Level: low

Activity Level: low

Materials: game sheet, pencils

Setup

For each player, make a copy of the game sheet provided.

How to Play

Players take turns saying a letter that they both write on their game sheets in a box of their choice. Letters can be repeated at the discretion of the players. After all of the boxes are filled, players score a point for each three-letter word they formed vertically, horizontally, and diagonally.

Variation

■ Use a 4 × 4 grid for players to create four-letter words. Play in the same manner, but only four-letter words score points.

Tips

■ Encourage students to circle words to aid in counting up the number of words created.

■ Use letter tiles to fill in spaces or laminate forms and use a dry-erase marker to reuse.

Three-Letter X Word Game Sheet

Four-Letter X Word Game Sheet

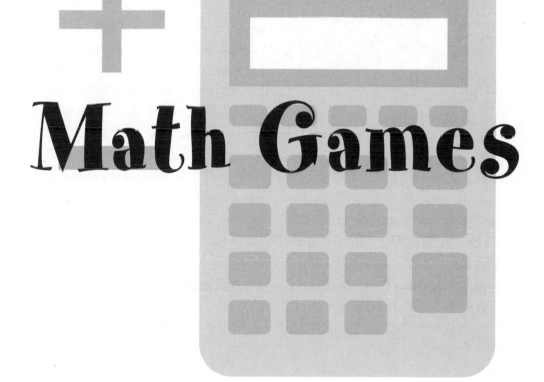

Math Games

Bake Me Some Pizza Pies

Using their knowledge of fractions, players collect pizza slices to complete a picture of their own pizza.

Age Range: 7 to 10

Skill Used: knowledge of fraction facts

Number of Players: 2 to 6

Noise Level: moderate

Activity Level: low

Materials: pizza drawings, paper pizza "pans" the size of the original pizza drawings, bag, die

Setup

Draw or find about twenty pictures of pizzas having the same diameter. Cut the pizzas into equivalent fractional parts such as 1/2, 1/4, 1/8, 1/12, 1/3, 1/6, and 1/9. There should be at least two or three pizzas cut in the same sized pieces so that they can fit together during the game. The fraction should be written on the back of each piece. Cut an equal number of paper pizza pans the same size as the pizzas.

How to Play

Before the start of the game, players decide if they are each going to make two or three pizzas; each player takes that number of pans. They also decide if the pieces must all be the same to complete a pie. This allows more advanced players to play together using equivalent fractions to mix pizza pieces to complete their pies. All of the pieces of pizza are placed in a bag. Players roll a die to determine how many pieces of pizza to pull out of the bag. The player draws the pieces and then tries to put fractional parts together on the pan to complete the pizzas. If a piece drawn is too big or can't be used, the player returns it to the bag and loses a turn.

After a player has finished placing the slices of pizza on the pans, that player tells how much pizza he or she has. "On this pan I have half a pizza and on this pan I have two-thirds of a pizza." Play then goes to the next player. The first person to fill all of his or her pizza pans wins.

Variations

■ For players just learning about fractions, divide the pans into equal fractional parts. Label each part with the fraction.

■ Make game pieces different types of pies such as pumpkin, apple, peach, and so on. Each type of pie can be cut to represent a different fraction. For example, an apple pie could be cut into halves and a pumpkin pie cut into eighths. Use aluminum pie plates for this variation.

Tips

....

■ Cut circles of equal size out of white paper. Pass the circles out to students and have them draw their favorite kinds of pizza. After mounting and laminating, cut these circles into fractional parts. Students enjoy seeing their own pizzas used as part of the game.

■ Purchase pizza cardboards from a pizza parlor to use as the pizza "pans" and pizza delivery boxes or take-out bags to hold the game pieces.

■ Enlarge pictures of divided circles from student textbooks or worksheets to use as patterns for cutting the pizzas.

Bean Soup

Players subtract one-digit numbers to determine how many beans to collect for their soup.

Age Range: 6 to 8

Skill Used: subtraction

Number of Players: 2

Noise Level: low

Activity Level: low

Materials: 4 sets of cards numbered from 1 to 10, assorted dried beans, container or bag

Setup

Prepare a pack of 40 cards by numbering them from 1 to 10 four times, or duplicate and cut out the sample cards. Place assorted beans in a bag or other container.

How to Play

To begin, place a container of beans between the players. The players deal out all of the cards and keep them facedown in piles in front of them. Players turn their top cards over at the same time. The player with the lower number takes from the container the number of beans equal to the difference between the numbers and gives them to the other player. For example, a 5 and a 3 are turned up. Since 5 − 3 = 2, the player with the 3 gives the other player 2 beans. If the numbers on the cards match, the players turn up their next cards to continue play.

The game ends when both players run out of cards. The winner is the one with the most beans.

Variation

■ Players turn their top cards over at the same time and take turns adding the numbers on the two cards together. The sum of the beans is taken by the player whose turn it is.

Tip

■ Give the players cups or little bowls to put their beans in during the game. This adds an element of mystery because a player can't see how many beans the other player has.

Bean Soup Cards

(Make four copies.)

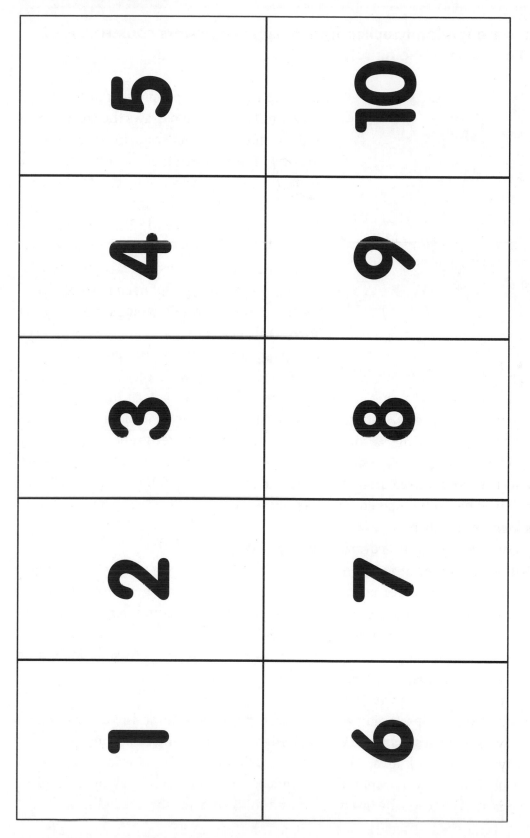

Bracelet Race

Plastic pop beads are randomly pulled from a bag, and players construct a bracelet that follows a sequencing rule.

Age Range: 5 to 8

Skills Used: sequencing, pattern knowledge

Number of Players: 2 to 5

Noise Level: moderate

Activity Level: low

Materials: cloth bag, plastic pop beads (minimum 16 per player), pattern strips (see samples), die

Setup

This game uses plastic toy beads that pop together to form strings and circles. Pattern strips should be prepared showing various design sequences of beads ranging from simple alternating colors to more complex designs using up to five colors. The design should be four or five beads long on the strip.

The pop beads should be separated and tossed in a cloth bag to begin the game. There should be at least 16 beads per player in the bag, but even more are recommended so that a single color doesn't run out during the game.

How to Play

To begin, place the pattern strips facedown on the table. Each player chooses a strip and places it faceup in his or her work area. The color placed on the left will be the start of the pattern, so the player must choose which way to orient the strip before play begins. The first player rolls the die and draws the corresponding number of beads from the bag without looking. Then, starting at the left side of the pattern strip, the player constructs the bead sequence following the rule shown. Beads that cannot be attached to the sequence are put back in the bag and play passes to the next player. Beads that are needed farther down the string cannot be kept but need to be returned to the container and drawn again on another turn. Only beads that are properly sequenced and popped together can be kept.

Play continues with the bead sequences showing a repeating pattern until the string is at least 16 beads long (or longer if it takes more to make the pattern repeat completely). When the pattern is complete, the player joins the beads in a circle to form a bracelet. The first player to complete a bracelet wins.

Variations

■ The game can be changed to the "Necklace Race," if that seems more interesting to both boys and girls. For necklaces, the number of beads may need to be increased, depending on the size of pop beads being used.

■ Some pop beads come in various shapes as well, and more complex sequences can be created using these. This variation will allow players to help themselves along by feeling around in the bag for the needed shapes.

■ An easier version of the game allows players to keep any bead that might fit in their sequence even if the bead cannot be immediately used in the pattern. This variation will speed up play.

■ Using pattern cards with words instead of pattern strips with colors makes the game more difficult and challenging for older players. For example, a card might read, "any alternating pattern of two colors" or "five different colored beads" or "alternating groups of one bead and three beads." Some sample pattern cards using words are provided.

■ Using letters instead of pictures on the pattern cards is a way to bring beginning algebra skills into the game. For example, a card might read "A, B, A, B" or "A, B, C, A, B, C," as shown in the sample pattern cards provided.

Tip
....

■ The target number of 16 beads was selected based on a common size of plastic pop bead. If the beads being used are extra large or significantly smaller, a different target number should be selected for a winning bracelet or necklace.

Bracelet Race Pattern Strips

(Color circles to show pattern.)

Bracelet Race Alternative Pattern Cards: Words

Any alternating pattern of two colors	Any alternating pattern of three colors
Any alternating pattern of five colors	A pattern of one, three
A pattern of one, two, three	All the same color
A pattern of four, two	A pattern of one, three, five
A pattern of three, two, one, two, three	Make up your own pattern.

Bracelet Race Alternative Pattern Cards: Letters

A, B, A, B	A, B, C, A, B, C
A, B, C, D, E, A, B, C, D, E	A, B, B, B, A, B, B, B
A, B, B, C, C, C, A, B, B, C, C, C	A, A, A
A, A, A, A, B, B, A, A, A, A, B, B	A, B, B, B, C, C, C, C, C, A, B, B, B, C, C, C, C, C
A, A, A, B, B, C, B, B, A, A, A	Make up your own pattern.

Bull's-Eye Feather Math

Using straws, players blow feathers around a bull's-eye game board to solve math facts.

Age Range: 7 to 12

Skill Used: knowledge of multiplication facts

Number of Players: 2 to 4

Noise Level: moderate

Activity Level: low

Materials: scorecards, feathers of different colors and patterns, pebbles, straws, pair of dice, game board (enlarged to 24" × 24")

Setup

Copy the scorecards provided or make your own and distribute to players. Scorecards should be prepared with 10 incomplete math problems on them, including: $0 \times \_ = \_$, $1 \times \_ = \_$, and so on. Using the pattern provided, create a single game board about 24" × 24" in size and label it with the same equations as those on the score sheets. The center of the game board, or bull's-eye, is the "Instant Win" space.

How to Play

Each player is given a scorecard, drinking straw, and a feather of his or her choice. Players use the feather for the entire game, so it must be obviously different from the others. Then the first player puts his or her feather at the edge of the circular game board. One gentle puff of air through the straw will move the feather to a spot on the board. Once the feather settles, the player anchors it with a small pebble and throws the dice. The total value of the roll is the number that substitutes for the blank found in that section of the game board. For example, if the feather falls on $4 \times \_$ and the roll is a total of 7, then the player solves the equation $4 \times 7 = 28$. This equation is filled in on that player's scorecard and play passes to the next player.

Rolls of 12 are considered "wild" and the player can choose any number to complete the problem and mark it off. If the answer given is incorrect, the player is told the correct answer, but his or her scorecard must remain blank for that equation. Then on the next turn, that player can choose to leave the feather on the same space and try again with a new roll of the dice or puff to a new spot. Landing outside the circle results in losing a turn, and that player begins his or her next turn at the outside edge of the game board.

Once the feather is on the board, the following turns go from the spot of the feather rather than the edge of the board. The player removes the pebble and puffs one time through the straw. The straw can be placed in any position for this, as long as the end doesn't touch the feather. All the feathers are anchored by pebbles during this game, except the one that is being used for a turn.

Players continue to take turns and fill in their scorecards. Landing on a space with an equation that has already been completed results in a lost turn for that player. The first one with a filled scorecard wins, unless the game ends early with a lucky landing on the "Instant Win" space.

Variation

■ The problems on the scorecards and game board can be changed to give practice with more facts.

Tip

■ Mark each feather with a very visible dot. If the feather covers two spaces when it lands, the player uses the space the dot falls upon. Players can dot their feathers themselves prior to starting. A bit of strategy comes into play this way as different parts of a feather might be easier or more difficult to control.

Bull's-Eye Feather Scorecards

Bull's-Eye Feather Scorecard

0 x _____ = _____

1 x _____ = _____

2 x _____ = _____

3 x _____ = _____

4 x _____ = _____

5 x _____ = _____

6 x _____ = _____

7 x _____ = _____

8 x _____ = _____

9 x _____ = _____

Bull's-Eye Feather Scorecard

0 x _____ = _____

1 x _____ = _____

2 x _____ = _____

3 x _____ = _____

4 x _____ = _____

5 x _____ = _____

6 x _____ = _____

7 x _____ = _____

8 x _____ = _____

9 x _____ = _____

Bull's-Eye Feather Scorecard

0 x _____ = _____

1 x _____ = _____

2 x _____ = _____

3 x _____ = _____

4 x _____ = _____

5 x _____ = _____

6 x _____ = _____

7 x _____ = _____

8 x _____ = _____

9 x _____ = _____

Bull's-Eye Feather Scorecard

0 x _____ = _____

1 x _____ = _____

2 x _____ = _____

3 x _____ = _____

4 x _____ = _____

5 x _____ = _____

6 x _____ = _____

7 x _____ = _____

8 x _____ = _____

9 x _____ = _____

Bull's-Eye Feather Math Game Board

(Enlarge to 24″ × 24″.)

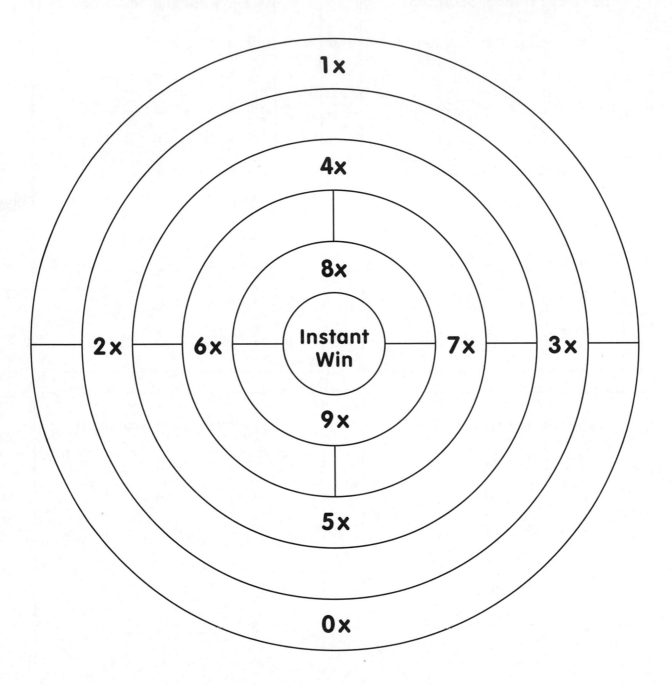

Buttons in a Box

Players toss a button in a marked box to land on numbered sections and add the values until they reach 100.

Age Range: 7 to 10
Skill Used: addition
Number of Players: 4
Noise Level: moderate
Activity Level: low to moderate
Materials: flat box, such as a soda case; button or token; pencil and paper

Setup

Draw lines dividing the bottom of the box into 10 equal sections. In each section, write a number from 0 to 9. Do not repeat any of the numbers.

How to Play

Players take turns tossing the button into the box. With each turn, the player who tossed the button scores the value of the space that it lands on. This score is added to that player's previous numbers until a sum of 100 is reached. If the button lands on a line, the player can toss the button again. The first one to reach 100 is the winner.

Variations

■ Divide the box into more sections. Sections can be labeled with higher numbers to provide practice in adding two-digit numbers. Additional sections can also be labeled with such consequences as: "Take an extra turn," "Choose any number from 1 to 10 to add on," "Subtract 10," and so on.

■ Turn this into a subtraction game by having the players start at 100 and count down to 0.

Tips

■ Depending on the skill level of the players, decide if they should use counters to reach 100 or if you want them to use calculators to check their addition after each throw.

■ Cut pieces of paper that fit exactly into the bottom of the box. Draw your sections and numbers on the paper so the same box can be used for different levels or can easily be traced for use in multiple game boxes.

Clock Race

Players move the hands of a clock according to the roll of a special die, trying to be the first to move from noon to midnight.

Age Range: 6 to 10
Skill Used: telling time
Number of Players: 2 to 4
Noise Level: low
Activity Level: low
Materials: clocks with moveable hands for each player, large wooden or foam die

Setup

Clocks with moveable hands can be made for this game using paper plates and hands held with paper fasteners. More elaborate clocks with gears can also be used if they are available.

The die for this game should be prepared to show these values on the sides: 30 minutes, 1 hour, 1 hour and 30 minutes, 2 hours, 2 hours and 30 minutes, and 3 hours. Foam cubes work best because the words can be large enough to be easily read.

How to Play

Each player is given a clock with moveable hands that are set to show 12 o'clock. The first player rolls the die and advances his or her clock by the amount of time shown. Players take turns moving the hands of their individual clocks. The first one to reach or pass 12 o'clock again wins.

Variations

■ If only one clock is available, have players pass it around the circle as they take their turns rolling the die and moving the hands. The player whose turn brings the hands to 12 o'clock exactly can be declared the winner.

■ This can become an elimination game by having the players drop out of the game when their individual clocks or their turn on the group's clock reaches or passes 12. The winner is the last player to move the hands.

Tip

■ Players with less experience and knowledge about telling time will do better with the geared clocks, as fewer mistakes will be made in advancing the hands.

Connect-O

Players compete to be the first to connect numbers in order that have been randomly scattered on a page.

Age Range: 5 to 6
Skill Used: number sequencing
Number of Players: 2 to 12
Noise Level: low to moderate
Activity Level: low
Materials: paper and pencil

Setup

None needed.

How to Play

To begin, each player writes the numbers 1 to 20 scattered randomly around a sheet of paper. Each number should be circled. The papers are turned facedown and passed to another player so that everyone has a sheet that someone else prepared. When the signal is given, the sheets are turned over and players draw lines between the circles to connect them in numerical order. The first player to connect all the circles says, "Connect-o!" and wins.

Variation

■ Instead of connecting numbers, players can write letters of the alphabet to put in order, words to put in alphabetical order, math problems with different answers to connect from high to low or low to high, and so on.

Tip

■ Have players include a star or other symbol on the first item in the sequence so everyone has an equal start.

Crazy Cuts

Players cut a standard index card, keeping it a single piece that is as long as possible when measured.

Age Range: 7 to 11

Skills Used: measuring length, strategic thinking

Number of Players: 2 to 8

Noise Level: moderate

Activity Level: moderate

Materials: index cards, scissors, yardstick

Setup

None needed.

How to Play

Each player is given an index card of the same size and scissors. The challenge is to cut the card to create a single long piece of paper. Folding the card is permitted, but any part of the card that is cut or torn off by accident cannot be included in the final measurement. No taping is allowed to increase the length of the final product. There is no time limit, but one can be implemented if it appears to be a problem for some groups of players.

Once cut, each piece is stretched along a yardstick and the length is recorded. The entries are judged by straight length, with the longest piece winning the challenge. Any long curved shapes should be stretched along the yardstick to measure them and scored based on the straight measurement. If the piece tears during measurement, the remainder is measured and that is the final score for that player. The player with the longest piece is the winner.

Variations

■ Players could roll a die to determine a specific number of cuts to make for a round of "Crazy Cuts."

■ Additional competitions can be done with larger rectangular cards or die-cut shapes such as stars or circles.

Tips

■ Each player should measure his or her own piece while the others watch. This eliminates the problem of someone else accidentally tearing a potential winner's piece.

■ This game becomes more interesting each time it is played. At first, players might just cut a strip the length of the card and be beaten by someone creative enough to cut a diagonal strip. Later plays of the game will lead to cuts of spirals, zigzags, and folded pieces that yield a much longer length.

■ Winning shapes could be displayed on a "Hall of Fame" with the measurement posted. This can make the game an ongoing challenge to unseat the current winner.

Dice-O

Players roll one to three dice, add the values, and cover that number on their bingo-style cards until a row of five is obtained.

Age Range: 8 to 10
Skill Used: addition
Number of Players: 2 to 6
Noise Level: low to moderate
Activity Level: low
Materials: game cards, 4 dice, tokens

Setup

Copy and use the sample game card or make your own 5 × 5 card with spaces numbered randomly from 1 to 24. Include a free space in the middle.

How to Play

Each player starts with a game card and a pile of tokens to use. Everyone places a token in the "Free" space. The player selected to go first rolls one, two, three, or all four dice as desired and adds up the values shown. If that number appears on his or her game card, a token is placed on that spot and play passes to the next person. If the number is not on the card, no token is placed and play passes anyway. The first player to have five tokens in a row, either across, up, down, or horizontally, shouts, "Dice-o!" and is the winner.

Variation

■ Write products for the multiplication facts 1 to 6 on the game cards. Play as previously described but with two dice, multiplying the numbers that turn up and covering the product if it appears on the card.

Tips

■ Allow players to cover a space no matter who rolls the dice for a speedy version of this game.

■ Give players blank game cards and allow them to make their own personal game card by writing in numbers from 1 to 24.

Dice-O Game Card

D	I	C	E	-O
		Free		

Down the Hall and Up the Elevator

Players use ordered pairs to be the first to get three tokens in a row, either horizontally or vertically.

Age Range: 8 to 10

Skill Used: understanding of ordered pairs

Number of Players: 2 to 4

Noise Level: low

Activity Level: low

Materials: game board, pair of dice, several same-colored tokens for each player

Setup

Copy the game board provided or make a 6 × 6 grid with numbers on each axis. Decorate it to look like a hotel with each space on the grid being a room.

How to Play

Each player selects an individual token color. The first player rolls the dice and decides what order to place the dice next to each other to create an ordered pair. The player moves his or her token to that space on the grid, or the hotel, by going "down the hall and up the elevator" or, in other words, across the lower axis and then up. If an ordered pair lands on a room that is already occupied, the player loses the turn and the dice are passed to the next player. The winner is the first one to get three markers in a row either horizontally or vertically.

Variations

■ Have players put tokens on more than three neighboring "rooms" vertically or horizontally to win. This can be left to chance by rolling the dice.

■ Change one axis from numbers to letters to correspond to a map grid. Make corresponding dice.

Tip

■ If time runs out for the game, the winner can be the one with the most markers in a row or with the most markers on the game board.

Down the Hall and Up the Elevator Game Board

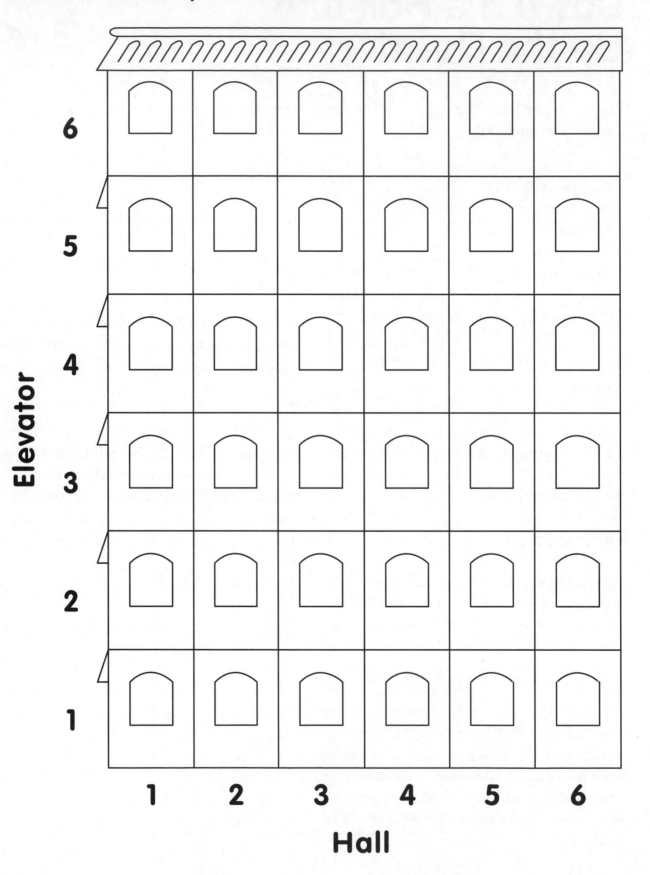

Egg Money

Eggs containing coins are chosen from a carton as players try to find the ones that match the amounts on the cards they've drawn.

> **Age Range:** 6 to 8
> **Skills Used:** knowledge of coin values, addition, memory
> **Number of Players:** 2 to 3
> **Noise Level:** moderate
> **Activity Level:** low
> **Materials:** egg carton, 12 plastic eggs, egg money cards, coins, small paper cups

Setup

Copy and cut apart the sample money cards or prepare your own. There should be at least four cards made for each money amount. Different formats for writing the amounts can be included in the deck as well.

Prepare 12 plastic eggs to contain different combinations of coins that add up to the amounts represented on the cards. These eggs are randomly placed in an egg carton. Distribute small paper cups to each player.

How to Play

Put the stack of egg money cards facedown within easy reach of all players. The first player chooses a card and then selects any egg from the carton to open. The player counts the coins aloud and announces the total. If the coins found in the egg add up to the amount on the card, the coins are removed and placed in the player's cup. Once matched, the card is displayed for all to see. The empty egg is not put back in the carton, but put aside for the rest of the game. If the egg contains the wrong amount of money, the egg is closed and returned to the box with the coins inside.

Players take turns trying to match an egg's amount to their cards. Once they have a match, they may take another card from the pile and try to find that amount of money. Each player must match the card that he or she has selected before taking another card and trying for another amount of money. The exception to this rule comes when both eggs containing a given amount have been found and a player holds or draws that duplicate card. In this case, the player discards and chooses another to match without losing a turn.

When all the eggs have been opened and emptied, the game is over and players count their money. The one with the most money is the winner.

Variations

■ Playing a set number of rounds or to a time limit makes this game quicker to play. The winner is still the player with the most money in his or her cup at the end of the time limit or number of turns.

■ Letting the players shake the eggs before choosing one makes this game noisier but a bit more playful. It can also help build awareness that more coins do not necessarily mean more money. Intentionally putting more coins in the lower value eggs adds this twist to the game.

Tip

- Keep a key showing the coins that go into each egg to start the game so that setting up for the next time is easy. Suggested groupings include:

5 cents = 1 nickel/5 pennies
10 cents = 10 pennies/2 nickels
25 cents = 5 nickels/2 dimes and 5 pennies
35 cents = 1 quarter and 1 dime/ 3 dimes and 1 nickel
50 cents = 2 quarters/4 dimes and 2 nickels
60 cents = 2 quarters and 1 dime/ 3 dimes and 6 nickels

Egg Money Cards
(Make at least two copies.)

$.05	$.10	$.25
$.35	$.50	$.60
5¢	10¢	25¢
35¢	50¢	60¢

50 or Bust!

Players use number cards to create equations with a value as close to 50 as possible without going over.

Age Range: 9 to 12

Skills Used: knowledge of addition, subtraction, multiplication, and division of whole numbers

Number of Players: 2 to 24

Noise Level: low

Activity Level: low

Materials: deck of number cards, set of math operation cards for each player

Setup

Copy and use the number cards provided to make a deck of cards using numbers from 1 to 9. There must be at least four cards per player. For example, if there are six players, the deck should have a minimum of 24 cards numbered from 1 to 9, for eight players, 32 cards are needed, and so on.

Make and give a set of math operation cards for each player.

How to Play

One player deals four cards to each player. Players use those four number cards and their choice of three operation cards to create an equation that is equal to or is as close to 50 without going over. Each player shares his or her equation and answer. The winner is the one with an answer equaling 50 or the closest answer to 50 without going over and "busting."

Variation

■ Add a wild card to the deck. A player getting the wild card can choose to make it any number from 1 to 9.

Tips

■ Let players use a calculator to follow along as each equation and answer is read.

■ Keep track of players' answers. Use these numbers to find range, mean, median, and mode for each round of the game.

■ Let students work in pairs.

50 or Bust! Number Cards

(Make enough copies so you have at least four cards per player.)

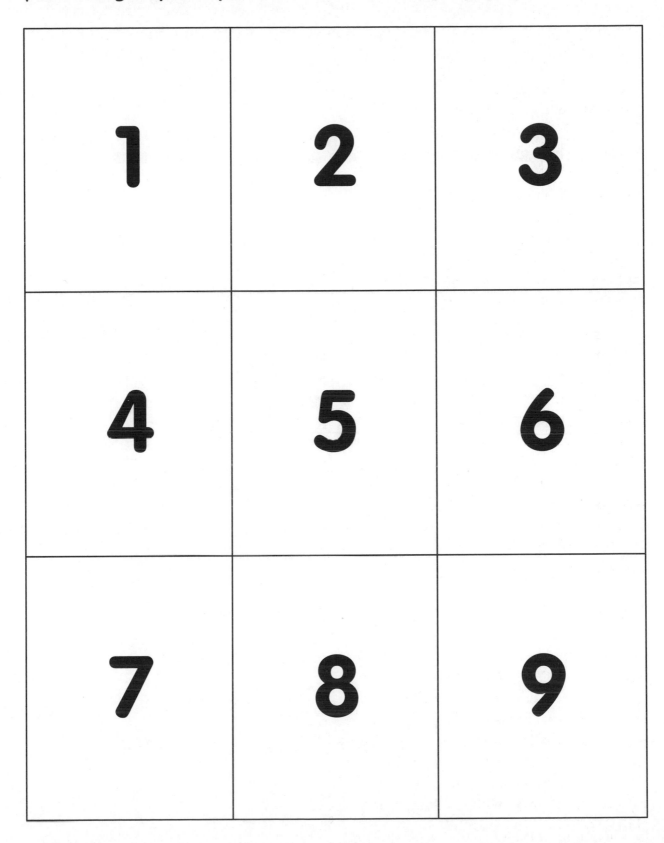

50 or Bust! Operation Cards

(Two sets of operation cards)

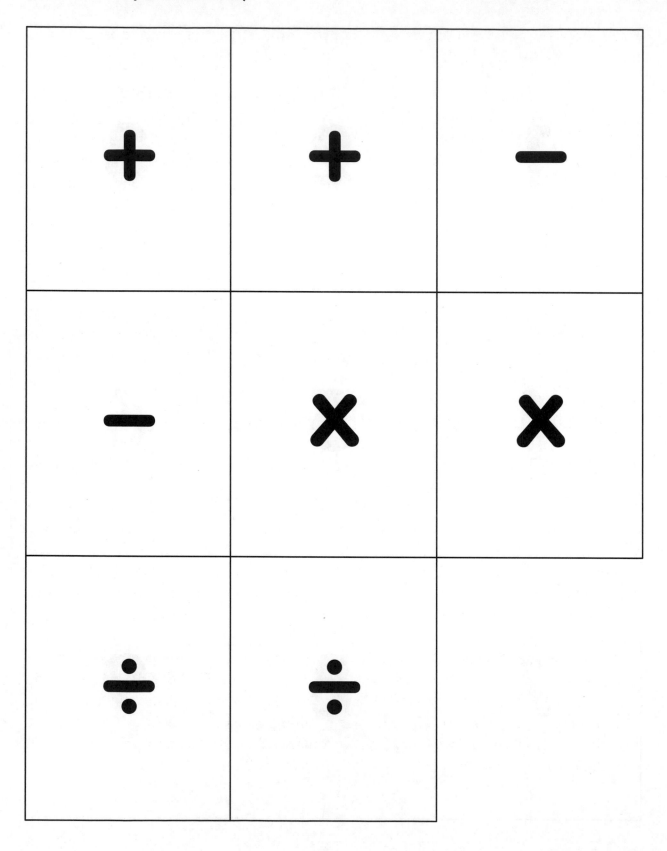

Got the Time?

Players collect sets of cards from each other that show the same time, but in different ways.

> **Age Range:** 6 to 9
> **Skills Used:** telling time, reading
> **Number of Players:** 3 to 5
> **Noise Level:** low
> **Activity Level:** low
> **Materials:** time cards

Setup

Prepare cards to show the time in three formats: analog, digital, and in words, or copy and use the time cards provided. The basic game can have 12 sets of these three types of cards using full hours.

How to Play

This game is played similar to Go Fish. Five cards are dealt to each player. Players who find any matching set of three in their hand can immediately put these cards on the table and draw replacements before the game begins. Extra cards are left facedown in the middle of the table.

The first player chooses any other player and asks for a specific card that goes with a card in his or her hand. Questions might be: "Do you have the digital six o'clock?" "Do you have the words for ten o'clock?" or "Do you have the clock face that shows one o'clock?"

Players must give the card that is requested if they are holding it. The player asking for cards can continue to ask for cards from any player as long as the requests are successful. Any sets collected this way are placed on the table and counted as one point. If the player doesn't have the requested card, he or she says, "Time out." The asker then chooses a card from the middle and his or her turn is over.

Players continue to take turns asking each other for cards until a player runs out of cards. The winner is the one who has collected the most sets.

Variations

■ Add cards to include times on the half hour and quarter hour.

■ The questions can be modified to be more general, as in "Do you have any four o'clocks?" The person being asked then must surrender all of the applicable cards at once. This variation can speed up the game.

■ For younger players who may not read the word cards as well, the game can be modified to include only the analog and digital cards. Adding a card that pictures a broken clock makes the game suitable for use with Old Maid rules.

Got the Time? Cards

1:00		**One o'clock**
2:00		**Two o'clock**
3:00		**Three o'clock**
4:00		**Four o'clock**
5:00		**Five o'clock**
6:00		**Six o'clock**

7:00		**Seven o'clock**
8:00		**Eight o'clock**
9:00		**Nine o'clock**
10:00		**Ten o'clock**
11:00		**Eleven o'clock**
12:00		**Twelve o'clock**

Hang Ten

Players turn over number cards to find pairs that add up to 10.

Age Range: 6 to 8
Skill Used: addition
Number of Players: 2
Noise Level: low
Activity Level: low
Materials: number cards

Setup

Make 18 surfboard-shaped number cards numbered from 1 to 9 twice, or use the sample number cards provided.

How to Play

Players lay the cards out facedown, Concentration-style. The players alternate turning over two cards. If the sum of the two cards equals 10, that player takes those cards and gets another turn. If the cards don't equal 10, the player says, "Wipe out!" The cards are turned back over, and it becomes the other player's turn. After all the matches are made, the player with more cards wins.

Variation

■ Add a "Hang Ten" surfboard card to the pack. Use this card as a wild card. When a player turns up the "Hang Ten" card, a match is created if the player can tell the number it should represent to equal 10.

Tip

■ To help younger players remember the goal of the game, place a card labeled "Hang 10" in full view of both players.

Hang Ten Number Cards

(Make two copies.)

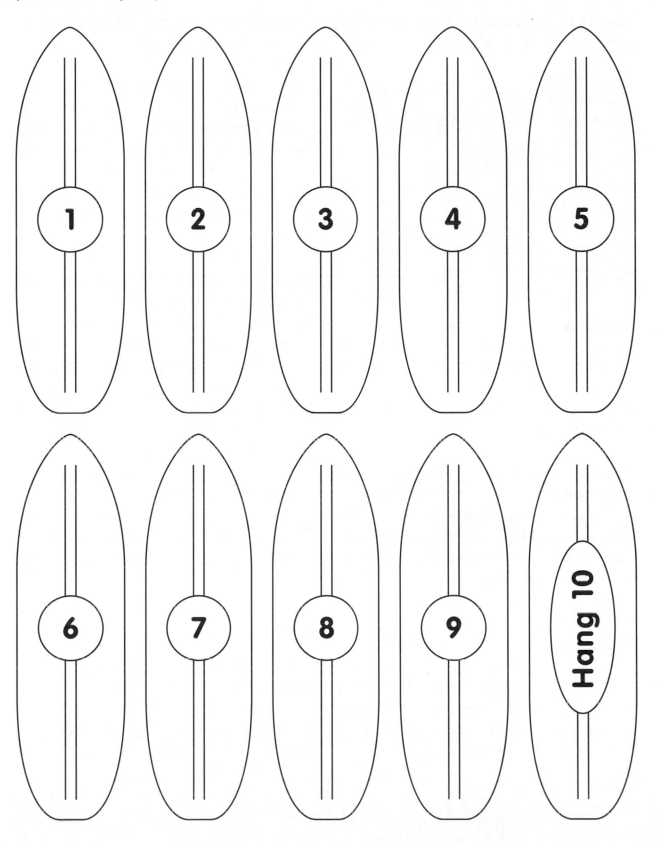

In or Out?

Players accumulate points from rolls of the dice but have to decide whether to keep rolling and risk losing it all if the "Hot Number" comes up.

Age Range: 8 to 12

Skills Used: addition, understanding of probability

Number of Players: 3 to 24

Noise Level: low to moderate

Activity Level: moderate

Materials: die (use more than one for increased difficulty), paper and pencil

Setup

Make a copy of the score sheet provided for each player or create your own.

How to Play

Distribute a score sheet to each player. The game director also draws the score sheet on the board or projects a copy of it on a screen. The die is rolled to establish the initial Hot Number, which is recorded in the Hot Number column on the chart.

All the players stand up. The game director rolls the die. If the first roll matches the Hot Number, then no one scores any points, and a new round is started using a new Hot Number rolled by the game director. If the number rolled doesn't match the Hot Number, everyone records the number in the Numbers Rolled space on their score sheet.

Each time a number is recorded, players get the chance to stay in or opt out. When they choose to go out, they sit down and add the values of the rolls they have recorded. The sum goes in the Round Total column. Players who stay in continue to accumulate numbers toward their total unless the Hot Number comes up.

When the Hot Number is rolled, all the players who are still standing get zero points for that round. The round ends when everyone is sitting or the Hot Number is rolled. Begin the next round with a roll of the die to establish a new Hot Number. Continue play in the same manner with the players determining when they want to keep the points or continue on. After five rounds, players total up their scores from each round. The highest total wins.

Variation

■ Use a pair of dice for multiplication, or multiply all single die answers by a certain number.

Tips

■ Use a 10-sided die to give players practice in adding higher numbers, too.

■ Do one round each day of the week, with the winner determined on Friday.

In or Out? Score Sheet

In or Out? Score Sheet		
Hot Number	**Numbers Rolled**	**Round Total**
	Grand Total	

In or Out? Score Sheet		
Hot Number	**Numbers Rolled**	**Round Total**
	Grand Total	

Let's Go Shopping!

Players have a set budget and try to buy items that equal that amount.

Age Range: 7 to 12

Skills Used: addition, subtraction

Number of Players: 2 to 24

Noise Level: low to moderate

Activity Level: low to moderate

Materials: shopping fliers from newspapers, catalogs, timer, pencil and paper, play money (optional)

Setup

Have a number of shopping fliers and catalogs available. Decide if the game will be played by individuals, pairs, or teams.

How to Play

Give players a set amount of money to spend that is appropriate to the age group and skill level of the players. This amount is the "goal amount." Announce the time limit they have to find and cut out money amounts from the fliers and catalogs that will get them as close as possible to the goal amount without going over. At the end of the time, players share their purchases and amounts of money remaining with the others. The player, pair, or team closest to the goal amount, without going over, is the winner.

Variations

■ Set a purpose for the shopping trip, such as buying things for a birthday party, shopping for family Christmas gifts, decorating a tree house or fort, and so on. Give time for the players to make a poster or write a story about what they purchased and why.

■ Have players use "mental math" by having them round the amounts to reach the goal. Compare the rounded totals to actual totals.

■ Select a player to be the cashier. Give play money, equaling the goal amount, to each of the other individual players, pairs, or teams. Players use the play money to make their purchases with the cashier. The cashier makes the proper change and gives it to the players. Play continues until the time is up or no more purchases can be made. The player, pair, or team with the least money left wins.

Tips

■ Demonstrate and practice the method of adding up to a certain amount and subtracting down from that amount. Players have the option of using either method during the game, or they can be directed to use one method or the other.

■ Allow players to use a calculator to check accuracy or to speed up play.

Math Crossing

Players place number and operation cards on a game board grid to make equations that cross each other like a crossword puzzle.

Age Range: 8 to 12

Skill Used: equation building

Number of Players: 2 to 4

Noise Level: low

Activity Level: moderate

Materials: number/operation cards, game board

Setup

Cut 60 square cards. Write the numbers 0 to 9 on 40 of the cards and operation signs (+, −, ×, ÷, =) on the other 20 cards, or copy and use the cards provided. Using a large sheet of paper, make a game board marked with squares the same size as the cards. This game board grid should be about 20 squares on a side, but can be larger or even rectangular if desired.

How to Play

To begin play, the cards are scattered facedown on the table. Each player chooses seven cards for his or her hand without showing the cards to the others. The first player uses at least five cards to create a correct equation on the game board. If that player does not have an equa-tion in his or her hand, the player chooses an additional card and the turn passes to the next player. A play is scored by adding the values of all the numbers used in the equation, plus one point for every operation square. For example, a play of 2 + 6 = 8 would score 18 points. After a play, additional cards are drawn so that a player always has at least seven.

The equation can use more than five cards as long as it is correct. Once the first equation is on the board, the following players must connect their equations in a "crossword" fash-ion. Players can add to either or both ends of an existing equation. Players score the points that they put on the board as well as the ones that were on the board for that equation already. If the equation requires a two-digit number, two cards are used and they take two spaces on the board.

Play continues until any player uses all his or her cards and there are no more left to draw. The players with cards remaining must subtract the value of those cards from the points they accumulated during the game. The player with the highest score wins.

Variation

■ Add cards with parentheses, decimal points, or fractions to the deck.

Tips
· ·

■ Have a calculator and scrap paper handy for players to check their answers and challenge the plays of the others.

■ If a challenger identifies and corrects an equation, he or she scores one point for each card in the equation, and the player who made that incorrect equation loses all his or her points for that equation.

Math Crossing Cards

(Make four copies.)

5	0	=
4	9	÷
3	8	×
2	7	−
1	6	+

Measure Up

Players search the area to find items matching a selected measurement. Winning items are the closest to the predetermined measurement.

Age Range: 6 to 12

Skills Used: measuring length, estimation

Number of Players: 2 to 10

Noise Level: moderate to high

Activity Level: moderate to high

Materials: cards with measurement terms, die, timer, ruler, yard and/or meter stick, tape measure, graduated cylinders, kitchen scale

Setup

Make one copy of the Measure Up record sheet and several copies of the provided Measure Up cards. Make these two-sided cards by writing a measurement term such as inch, foot, liter, ounce, and so on on the front of the card. Write all linear measurements in one color, volume measurements in another color, and mass measurements in a third color. Different colors or underlining can be used to differentiate metric and standard measurement terms. On the back of each card, list the numbers 1 through 6. After each number, write a measurement amount for that unit or term that is age appropriate for the players to find. For example, the front side of the card might have "ounces" written on it. The list side of the card for an 8- or 9-year-old could show: 1 ounce, 6 ounces, 8 ounces, 16 ounces, 18 ounces, and 24 ounces in the spaces marked 1 to 6.

How to Play

A game director is chosen. This person is in charge of the cards, the timer, the record sheet, and verifying measurements. The game director fans the cards out and offers them to the first player. That player draws a measurement card and reads the unit of measure to all the players. The next player rolls the die. The player with the card reads the amount on the back of the card that corresponds to the number on the die. (Using the setup example, the first player would announce, "Ounces." If the second player rolled a 4, "16 ounces" would be said.) The game director sets the timer for three minutes. All the players hunt around the area to find an item that matches the measurement—in this example something that would equal 16 ounces. The item is taken to the game director and the player measures the item. The player's name, the object, and the measurements are recorded. When the timer goes off or all students have found and measured their items, the player who found the item closest to the predetermined measurement wins.

Tips

• •

■ Set guidelines for where players can find items. Maybe they can only find items from their desks. Maybe they can use items from common areas of the room. Or a container of assorted items can be provided with this game. Certain areas that might be off limits could be a special display, a learning center, and so on.

■ After a player has his or her item measured and recorded, that player can assist other players in locating an item.

■ Be sure players have time to see, feel, and compare their items with the winning item.

Measure Up Cards

(Cut cards on horizontal lines. Fill in information. Fold in half. Laminate.)

(Front of the card)   *(Back of the card)*

1. _____
2. _____
3. _____
4. _____
5. _____
6. _____

_____

1. _____
2. _____
3. _____
4. _____
5. _____
6. _____

_____

1. _____
2. _____
3. _____
4. _____
5. _____
6. _____

_____

Measure Up Record Sheet

Find an item that is _____ .

	Student's Name	Item Found	Measurement
1.			
2.			
3.			
4.			
5.			
6.			
7.			
8.			
9.			
10.			
11.			
12.			
13.			
14.			
15.			
16.			
17.			

Move It Right, Move It Left

Players try to be the first to reach +10 or −10 on a number line by drawing numbers and moving a token.

Age Range: 7 to 12

Skills Used: understanding of positive and negative numbers

Number of Players: 2 to 6

Noise Level: low

Activity Level: low

Materials: number line from −10 to +10, game cards, cloth bag, token for each player

Setup

Prepare a number line that goes from −10 to +10. Copy the game cards provided. Or, write numbers from −9 to +9 on paper, making duplicates of −3 through +3. Make additional consequence slips, including "Return to 0," "Trade places with another player," "Take another turn," "Move to +10 or −10 for an automatic win," and "Move 2 spaces in either direction." Place cards in the bag.

How to Play

Each player starts by placing a token on 0 on the number line. The first player draws a card from the bag and moves his or her token that number of spaces. The card is returned to the bag. The next player draws a card and play continues. If the number drawn will move a player's token off the number line, that move is not made. The game ends when a player lands on −10 or +10.

Variations

■ Make the game last longer by extending the number line in both directions.

■ Select a certain number to be the "hot number" to land on to win. Put out a card with that number or mark the positive and negative number space in some way.

Tips

■ Have students keep track of the number of turns they took in order to land on −10, +10, or the hot number. Graph or chart that information.

■ Make the number line on a large piece of paper, canvas, or plastic. Players become the tokens, walking on the number line as they make their moves.

Move It Right, Move It Left Game Cards

-9	-8	-7
-6	-5	-4
-3	-2	-1
0	1	2
3	4	5
6	7	8
9	1	-1
2	-2	3
-3	Return to 0.	Trade places with another player.
Take another turn.	Move 2 spaces in either direction.	Move to +10 or -10 for an automatic win!

On a Roll

Players add up rolls of the dice to get the highest score but risk having nothing if doubles come up.

Age Range: 7 to 10
Skill Used: addition
Number of Players: 2 to 8
Noise Level: moderate
Activity Level: low
Materials: pair of dice, pencil and paper, score sheet

Setup

Copy and distribute the score sheet shown to each player.

How to Play

Players take turns rolling two dice and adding the numbers. After the roll, each player decides whether to write down that sum or hope for a higher sum on the next roll. Once a player has chosen and written down a sum, it can't be changed. A round is done when doubles are rolled or all of the players have written down a number. Any player who hasn't written down a number prior to doubles being rolled scores zero points for that round. Play five rounds. At the end of five rounds, players add their five scores to come up with a grand total. The player with the highest grand total wins.

Variations

■ Follow the same game procedure, but this time players try to end up with the lowest score.

■ Subtract the numbers on the dice to try to end up with the lowest score. After five rounds, add the scores. The player with the lowest total wins.

■ Multiply the numbers on the dice to try to earn the highest score. After five rounds, add the scores. The player with the highest total wins.

Tips

■ Younger players can use calculators to determine their totals for all of the rounds.

■ Give each player cards numbered 2 through 12. When a player decides on a sum to keep, he or she holds up that card. When all of the players have made a choice, the next round begins.

On a Roll Score Sheet

On a Roll Score Sheet	
Round	**Sum**
1	
2	
3	
4	
5	
Grand Total	

On a Roll Score Sheet	
Round	**Sum**
1	
2	
3	
4	
5	
Grand Total	

On a Roll Score Sheet	
Round	**Sum**
1	
2	
3	
4	
5	
Grand Total	

On a Roll Score Sheet	
Round	**Sum**
1	
2	
3	
4	
5	
Grand Total	

Pebbles for the Pot

Players compare the cards that they turn up to determine how many pebbles to add to a partially filled jar of water. The player who causes the water to overflow wins the game.

Age Range: 7 to 9

Skill Used: subtraction

Number of Players: 2

Noise Level: moderate

Activity Level: low

Materials: pebbles, clear plastic jar (approximately 2 pints), standard deck of cards, paper towels

Setup

Remove all of the face cards from the deck and shuffle the remaining cards. Fill the jar about three-quarters with water, and place the jar on a paper towel. A generous pile of pebbles should be available, enough to cause the water to overflow if they are placed in the jar of water.

How to Play

Players deal out the whole deck of cards facedown. Players turn over their top cards and compare the numbers. With an ace being a low card, the player with the higher number subtracts the value of his or her opponent's card. The answer to the subtraction problem becomes the number of pebbles that the player with the higher card gently drops into the jar.

Play continues with the card values being subtracted and the difference determining the number of pebbles dropped in the jar until the water overflows. The player who puts in the pebble that causes the water to overflow wins the game.

Tip

■ A mark on the side of the jar is a helpful guide for filling the jar to begin this game based on your given set of pebbles.

Penny Pitch

Players take turns tossing pennies to land on the numbered squares of a calendar page.

> **Age Range:** 8 to 11
> **Skills Used:** addition, ability to use a calculator
> **Number of Players:** 2 to 4
> **Noise Level:** moderate
> **Activity Level:** moderate
> **Materials:** page from a calendar, pennies, score sheet, calculator for each player

Setup

Make copies of the score sheet provided, and give one to each player. Place the calendar page on the floor against a wall. Put a piece of tape on the floor to determine where players stand to toss their pennies.

How to Play

Each player gets an equal number of pennies to toss (from two to five). On each turn, players toss their pennies, one at a time, against a wall to rebound onto the calendar page. Players record the numbers that their pennies landed on and add the values to get a score, which they announce to their opponents. If any other player thinks the answer is wrong and proves it on a calculator, then the first player is out and has no score for that round. Players score zero if the penny misses the calendar page.

The game continues with players taking their pennies off the calendar and other players pitching their pennies. At the end of each round, players calculate their totals and record them on their score sheets. After each player has had an equal number of predetermined turns, the scores from all of the rounds are totaled and the player with the highest score wins.

Variations

■ This game can be played by teams. Play would alternate between the two teams with a different player tossing the pennies each round. The player who tossed the pennies adds the values, but the rest of the team can check and verify the answer before announcing it to the other team.

■ Give the players two or three nickels or dimes to toss. Players multiply the calendar number the coin lands on by the value of the coin.

Tips

■ To speed up the game, a player can toss all of the pennies at the same time.

■ If there isn't time for the players to play 10 rounds, let them save their score sheets for another time. Play can continue later with the same players, or add an element of luck and let new groups form to continue play.

■ Place the calendar page in a box to contain errant pennies.

Penny Pitch Score Sheet

Round	Numbers	Round Total	Game Total
1			
2			
3			
4			
5			
6			
7			
8			
9			
10			

Poison Pebble

Players take turns drawing pebbles from a pile using strategy to avoid taking the colored "poison pebble."

Age Range: 6 to 12

Skills Used: addition, knowledge of odd and even numbers, strategic thinking

Number of Players: 2 to 4

Noise Level: low to moderate

Activity Level: low

Materials: 50 small pebbles, pair of dice, game board, pencil and paper

Setup

Copy and use the game board provided or prepare your own game board having two equal areas labeled "odd" and "even." Gather 50 small pebbles. Paint one pebble a distinctive color to become the "poison pebble" while keeping the others their natural colors.

How to Play

One player is selected as the Pebble Master for the round and arranges the pebbles on the board with each one clearly placed in either the odd or even section. The poison pebble can be placed in either section. The number of pebbles in each section does not have to be equal. A section can be left empty or the poison pebble can be placed on its own if desired, for strategic reasons.

The first player rolls the dice. A sum of the roll equaling 3, 5, 7, 9, or 11 means pebbles are removed from the odd side of the board. A sum of the roll equaling 2, 4, 6, 8, 10, or 12 means pebbles are removed from the even side of the board. Players must remove at least one pebble after they roll, but not more than three pebbles, from the corresponding odd or even section of the board. Once pebbles are taken off by the player who rolled, his or her turn is over. Then the next player rolls the dice, continuing play in the same manner.

The round continues until one player is forced to take the poison pebble on his or her turn. The other players count their collected pebbles and keep a running tally of their scores. The player with the poison pebble has a score of zero for that round. Scores from the next rounds are added together. The first player to reach 100 wins the game.

Variation

■ Play the game in the same manner but with two poison pebbles.

Tip

■ Small objects that relate to a classroom theme or unit, such as plastic animals, toy food, and building blocks, can be substituted for the pebbles. Be sure the "poison" object can be easily identified.

Poison Pebble Game Board

Odd	Even

Polygon Crossing

Carpet remnants of various shapes are used to make a path across the play space, with players competing to get across first.

Age Range: 6 to 10

Skill Used: shape identification, strategic thinking

Number of Players: 4 to 8

Noise Level: moderate

Activity Level: moderate

Materials: carpet scraps or squares, foam die, masking tape, game key

Setup

This game uses an assortment of carpet remnants cut into shapes large enough for a player to stand on. A 12-inch square is a reasonable size. There should be at least 40 pieces in all, with at least six of each shape included in the set (square, rectangle, triangle, hexagon, and parallelogram). The pieces do not have to be exactly the same size or perfectly shaped to play this game.

The starting line and finish line for the game should be marked on the floor with masking tape. The distance between the lines should be eight times the dimension of the squares used in the game. For example, if the squares are 12″ × 12″, the two lines should be about 8 feet apart. The space marked should be wide enough for players to be able to stand side-by-side while playing, so a wider space is needed for a game with four teams.

A 6″ × 6″ foam cube is used for a die so that it can be easily seen by all players. The numbers 1 to 6 should be written on the faces.

How to Play

Four individual players or teams of two take their places at the taped starting line. A supply of shapes cut from carpet remnants are within easy reach. The team chosen to go first rolls the die and takes the corresponding shape from the pile as shown on the game key: 1—square, 2—triangle, 3—rectangle, 4—parallelogram, 5—hexagon, and 6—take a piece. Rolling a 6 allows the players on that team to take the end or last piece from any other team's path and put it on their own path. (This is not possible on the very first play since no shapes are on the board, so the starting team can roll again if a 6 comes up in that turn.)

The team uses the shape indicated by the die to begin a path from the starting line to the finish line. Once a shape is in a path, it can be stolen by a team rolling a 6. A flat side of the shape must be against the starting line. Teams take turns adding to their paths with each additional piece having a flat side matching up with the previous piece as the paths are constructed. Play continues with teams taking turns until one team wins by reaching the finish line with a shape touching or crossing the line. Players celebrate the victory with a ceremonial walk across the path.

Variation

■ Use pattern blocks or shapes cut from paper and an ordinary die to turn this into a table game. Colorful pieces add to appeal.

Polygon Crossing Key

Die	Carpet Shape
1	Square
2	Triangle
3	Rectangle
4	Parallelogram
5	Hexagon
6	Take a Piece

Pulling Strings

Players draw strings with hidden markings from a specially prepared can, measure the sections, and mark off the measurement on their game cards in an attempt to get a row of marked spaces and win.

Age Range: 7 to 10
Skill Used: measuring length
Number of Players: 2 to 6
Noise Level: low
Activity Level: low
Materials: coffee can with lid, strings, ruler, game cards, tokens, permanent markers

Setup

White cotton string works well for this game; it should be cut into at least 24 pieces, each about 15 inches long. Using a permanent marker, a middle section of the string is colored to be a particular measurement used in the game. Markings should be in full inch increments to 12 inches. There should be two strings prepared for each length used. The ends of the string can be trimmed within 2 inches of the marked section to make the smaller marked strings shorter and easier to handle. Six random strings should have one of their ends colored red.

Cut six or seven slits in a plastic coffee can lid. The lid is used to hold strings up so that players can pull one out at a time without seeing the markings. If the lid is transparent, it will need to be painted on the inside to conceal the strings in the can. The strings need to be put in place before the game starts with the red ends hidden.

Copy and distribute the game cards provided, or make your own 3 × 3 grids with measurements written in the nine squares (e.g., 1 inch, 2 inches, 3 inches, etc.). Each of the six game cards should be different from each other as shown and a collection of tokens is needed for markers on them.

How to Play

Players are each given a unique game card and the prepared coffee can is set out within easy reach. To begin, the first player pulls any string from the can and measures the length of the colored middle part with the ruler. If there is no red mark on the end, the player announces the measurement and all players who have that length on their cards can mark it with a token. If the red mark appears, only the player who pulled the string can mark his or her card. A player wins when he or she has three tokens in a line, as in tic-tac-toe.

Variations

■ This game can be made more difficult by using strings with finer measurements, such as 3½ inches, or by mixing inches and centimeters in the same game.

■ Game boards can also be enlarged to 4 × 4 grids or 5 × 5 grids.

■ Four other strings can be marked with green on the hidden end. When a player pulls a green string, only the other players are allowed to mark their cards.

■ A third color could be used to require the puller to remove the corresponding mark from his or her card.

Tips

■ To avoid fraying strings, use a drop of glue or a bit of tape on the ends.

■ Be sure to choose string that will not stretch and change length during the course of play.

Pulling Strings Game Cards

2 inches	**5** inches	**8** inches
7 inches	**4** inches	**3** inches
10 inches	**1** foot	**6** inches

1 foot	**9** inches	**6** inches
3 inches	**2** inches	**4** inches
8 inches	**7** inches	**1** inch

11 inches	**1** inch	**9** inches
3 inches	**7** inches	**5** inches
4 inches	**6** inches	**2** inches

1 foot	**1** inch	**11** inches
2 inches	**10** inches	**3** inches
9 inches	**4** inches	**8** inches

5 inches	**8** inches	**2** inches
4 inches	**1** foot	**7** inches
6 inches	**9** inches	**3** inches

5 inches	**8** inches	**2** inches
4 inches	**1** foot	**7** inches
6 inches	**9** inches	**3** inches

The Ruler Rules

Players total the measurement of common classroom objects to move 100 spaces on a game board.

Age Range: 7 to 10

Skills Used: Measuring length, addition

Number of Players: 4 to 24

Noise Level: moderate to high

Activity Level: high

Materials: rulers; cards with items to measure that are found in the game area; pencil, pen, or game piece for each team; chart, game board.

Setup

Create and make copies of cards with names of classroom items to measure. Examples of items could be the height of a flowerpot, the width of a specific magazine or book, the length of a remote control, the height of a chair, and so on. Additional cards can be made of items "planted" in the game area such as pens, specific toys, or even food. Make matching game boards, in either a chart or track format, numbered from 1 to 100 for each team.

How to Play

Divide the players into teams of 2 to 4. Each team draws a card from the pack and finds that object in the game area. Teams measure that object to the nearest unit with a ruler and write the answer on the card. The team returns to their game board and moves or marks the number of spaces equal to the measurement of the object. They draw another card and repeat the process. The first team to complete or move through all 100 spaces on the game board wins.

Variations

■ Eliminate the need for the game board by having each team add and record their measurements as they play. When they reach a total of 100, they win.

■ Have players or teams subtract or count down their measurements from 100.

Tips

■ Use a hundred chart as the game board for each team.

■ Take digital pictures of the objects to measure and glue them on the game cards.

■ Be sure to establish whether the team must move together from the game board area to the object and back again, or if they can split up and have a different player in charge of each step of the activity.

■ Everyone using rulers with a single unit of measure will cause less confusion, or place a sticker on the edge that will be used.

■ Special directions, such as "Go back 3 spaces," "Skip ahead 2," or "You rule, double your next measurement," can be added to various spaces on the game board or can be hidden in the pack of cards.

■ When making up the cards of items to measure, consider how long you want the game to last. Choose smaller items to make the game last longer and larger things for a quicker game.

Secret Message

Players color squares containing select numbers to reveal a letter. After completing several squares, the letters are put in order to tell a secret message.

Age Range: 5 to 7

Skills Used: number recognition, listening, early reading

Number of Players: 2 to 10

Noise Level: low

Activity Level: low

Materials: individual hundred charts, crayons

Setup

Choose a short word the players will be able to read and act out, such as *hop, sit,* and *cry*. Use the blank hundred chart provided to make a key for the game director by lightly shading squares to form the letters of the target word. The numbers must remain visible in the key. The letters of the word will be in a scrambled order on the key. A sample key for the word *sit* is shown.

How to Play

Players listen as a number is called by the game director. Players are to color the corresponding square on their own sheet. The caller continues listing numbers as players color to reveal one secret letter at a time.

Continue in this manner until all of the letters of the word have been revealed. Once that is accomplished, the players try to form the secret word with the letters. The first one who says and acts out the correct word is the winner.

Variation

■ Let the students color squares to draw a picture or a single letter or number. Choose a drawing and allow that player to call the numbers for the other students.

Tips

■ Have the students use game markers first so work can easily be checked for accuracy prior to players coloring in the spaces.

■ To make the game more exciting, tell players the category of the hidden object (design, letter, number) and let them predict what it will be.

Secret Message Hundred Chart

1	2	3	4	5	6	7	8	9	10
11	12	13	14	15	16	17	18	19	20
21	22	23	24	25	26	27	28	29	30
31	32	33	34	35	36	37	38	39	40
41	42	43	44	45	46	47	48	49	50
51	52	53	54	55	56	57	58	59	60
61	62	63	64	65	66	67	68	69	70
71	72	73	74	75	76	77	78	79	80
81	82	83	84	85	86	87	88	89	90
91	92	93	94	95	96	97	98	99	100

Secret Message Key

(Target word is *sit*.)

1	2	3	4	5	6	7	8	9	10
11	12	13	14	15	16	17	18	19	20
21	22	23	24	25	26	27	28	29	30
31	32	33	34	35	36	37	38	39	40
41	42	43	44	45	46	47	48	49	50
51	52	53	54	55	56	57	58	59	60
61	62	63	64	65	66	67	68	69	70
71	72	73	74	75	76	77	78	79	80
81	82	83	84	85	86	87	88	89	90
91	92	93	94	95	96	97	98	99	100

Speed Limit

As they choose cards, players move their toy cars along a game board toward the 65 mph limit.

Age Range: 7 to 10

Skills Used: addition, subtraction

Number of Players: 2 to 6

Noise Level: moderate

Activity Level: low

Materials: speed limit cards, toy cars or laminated pictures of cars, game board, paper and pencil

Setup

As shown, make a game board that is a rectangle large enough for all the toy cars to be placed in the section marked "Parking Lot." The remainder of the board has lines equally spaced with the markings "5 mph," "10 mph," and so on—up to "65 mph" just before the section marked "Speeding!"

Make your own speed limit cards or copy and use the cards provided. These cards include "speed up" cards for 5, 10, 15, 20, 25, and 30 miles per hour, with more cards showing the lower speeds than the higher speeds. "Speed up 5 miles per hour" should be the most common card. There are also "slow down" cards for 5, 10, and 15 miles per hour. Cards reading "Hit the brakes" and "Change lanes" should also be mixed in. There should be enough cards for every player to get at least 10 turns, so a game for six players would need a stack of at least 60 cards. Two police cards showing a police car should also be mixed in.

How to Play

Each player chooses a unique toy car or picture of a car to be his or her game piece. These are put behind the starting line. The cards are shuffled and placed facedown. The player who is selected to go first takes a card from the top of the stack and moves his or her car the correct number of spaces to indicate that player's speed. Play continues with players choosing cards and moving their cars accordingly.

"Hit the brakes" sends the car back to the parking lot. "Change lanes" means that the car stays at the same speed and does not advance or move back on the board for that turn. The police car card allows the player to choose to make any other player "pull over" and stop, which sends that player back to the parking lot. Players can use scrap paper to add or subtract speeds and determine the correct location on the board for their cars.

Players may not go over the speed limit of 65 miles per hour. To win, cars must reach 65 but not go over. If a card cannot be used without violating the speed limit, it is discarded faceup and play passes to the next person. The next player has the option of using the top card from the discard pile or taking one from the facedown pile. The first player to get exactly to the speed limit of 65 miles per hour wins.

Tip

· ·

■ Using toy cars makes the game more interesting and motivating, but there is a chance that it can become noisier as well. Pictures cut from magazines can be laminated to make attractive game tokens as an alternative.

Speed Limit Game Board

Speeding!

65 mph

60 mph

55 mph

50 mph

45 mph

40 mph

35 mph

30 mph

25 mph

20 mph

15 mph

10 mph

5 mph

Parking Lot

Speed Limit Cards

(Make multiple copies depending on group size.)

Speed up 5 mph.	Speed up 10 mph.	Speed up 30 mph.	Change lanes.	
Speed up 5 mph.	Speed up 10 mph.	Speed up 25 mph.	Slow down 15 mph.	Hit the brakes.
Speed up 5 mph.	Speed up 10 mph.	Speed up 20 mph.	Slow down 10 mph.	Hit the brakes.
Speed up 5 mph.	Speed up 10 mph.	Speed up 15 mph.	Slow down 5 mph.	Change lanes.

Sum Big Fish

Players try to combine the cards they are dealt into equations equaling 10.

Age Range: 6 to 9

Skill Used: addition

Number of Players: 2 to 6

Noise Level: low

Activity Level: low

Materials: pack of 44 cards numbered 0 to 10 four times

Setup

Prepare a pack of 44 cards by numbering them from 0 to 10 four times, or copy and cut out the number cards supplied.

How to Play

Choose one player to be the dealer. That person deals four cards to each player. The extra cards are placed in a pile in the "pond" (the middle). First, players check their hands and lay down any combinations of cards totaling 10. Replacement cards are drawn from the pond in order to have four cards when play begins. Players take turns asking any other player for a specific number that, when added to the cards they currently hold, would make a sum of 10. Sums can be made from more than two cards, for example, 3 + 4 + 3. If the person asked doesn't have the requested card, the player takes a card from the pond and it becomes the next player's turn. If the person has the requested card, it is given to the player who requested it. Then, that card, along with the other ones, is laid down and the equation that equals 10 is stated. The game ends when one player runs out of cards. The one with the most cards laid down wins.

Tip

■ Use fish-shaped cards to make this game more interesting.

Sum Big Fish Number Cards

0	0	0	0
1	1	1	1
2	2	2	2
3	3	3	3
4	4	4	4
5	5	5	5

Sum Big Fish Number Cards (continued)

6	6	6	6
7	7	7	7
8	8	8	8
9	9	9	9
10	10	10	10

Sum of the String

Players take turns pulling a multicolored string from a coffee can to earn points.

> **Age Range:** 7 to 11
> **Skills Used:** addition, knowledge of place value
> **Number of Players:** 2 to 4
> **Noise Level:** moderate
> **Activity Level:** low
> **Materials:** coffee can with plastic lid, yarn in four colors (white, red, green, and blue), paper and pencils, standard deck of playing cards

Setup

The red, green, and blue yarn should be cut into lengths of about 8 to 12 inches with at least 10 pieces of each color. Only one piece of white yarn is needed. The pieces do not have to be exactly the same length for this game. The colored pieces should be knotted together in a random order to form a multicolored string. The same color can be tied to itself. This knotted string is rolled up and put in a coffee can. The end of the multicolored string should be knotted to the piece of white yarn, forming the starting end.

Put the cover on the can with the end of the white string showing through a slit in the cover. As shown in the key, each of the three colors of string represents a particular place value: green is the ones place, blue is the tens place, and red is the hundreds place.

Before the game, shuffle a deck of playing cards with the 10s and face cards removed.

How to Play

The player chosen to go first takes a card from the top of the deck and pulls the white string just until the next knot appears and reveals the color of the next section. The players do not use the color that is showing in subsequent turns because that was the last player's string. The color of the string after the knot determines the place value of the card number and the player records it on his or her paper. For example, a 6 card and the color blue would correspond to the number 60.

As play continues around the group, players add numbers to their cumulative total. The first player to reach or pass 1,000 points is the winner.

Variation

■ Additional place values can be added by including more colors in the knotted string. The target total would be adjusted upward to be the value just above the highest place value in the string. For example, if there are five colors in the string, then the winning total is 100,000 points.

Tips

■ Montessori math materials use the colors mentioned in the game key (green, blue, and red), and the repetition can be helpful for younger players.

■ If players begin to predict the order of the colors on the string, reverse it or cut and tie it back together in a new arrangement to keep the game fresh.

■ Players can use a calculator to check their answers.

Sum of the String Key

Red	Blue	Green
Hundreds	Tens	Ones

Sum Thinking

Players use strategy to fill in blanks that appear in equations and win with the highest total.

Age Range: 8 to 12

Skills Used: addition, strategic thinking

Number of Players: 2 to 6

Noise Level: low

Activity Level: low

Materials: set of cards numbered 0 to 9 twice, response sheet, pencil

Setup

Make a deck of cards numbered from 0 to 9 twice, using the cards provided or making your own. Make copies of the response sheet for each player.

How to Play

The game begins with the players sitting in a circle. The deck of number cards is facedown in the middle within easy reach. Players take turns turning over a card and saying the number. After each number is announced, all of the players decide where to write the number in the first section (the two-digit problem) of their own response form. When the correct number of cards plus one (that is five numbers for the two-digit problem) have been read, players solve their problems. The extra number is needed so that a "throwaway number" can be chosen. Choosing where to write the numbers, and which number is best to throw away, determines the total obtained in the round. The player with the highest sum wins the round.

Continue playing in the same manner for the three-digit problem and then the four-digit problem. Find the winner for each round. The player with the highest grand total for the three problems becomes the grand champion.

Variation

■ Play the game in the same manner, but the player with the lowest sum wins.

Sum Thinking Number Cards

0	0	1	1
2	2	3	3
4	4	5	5
6	6	7	7
8	8	9	9

Sum Thinking Response Sheet

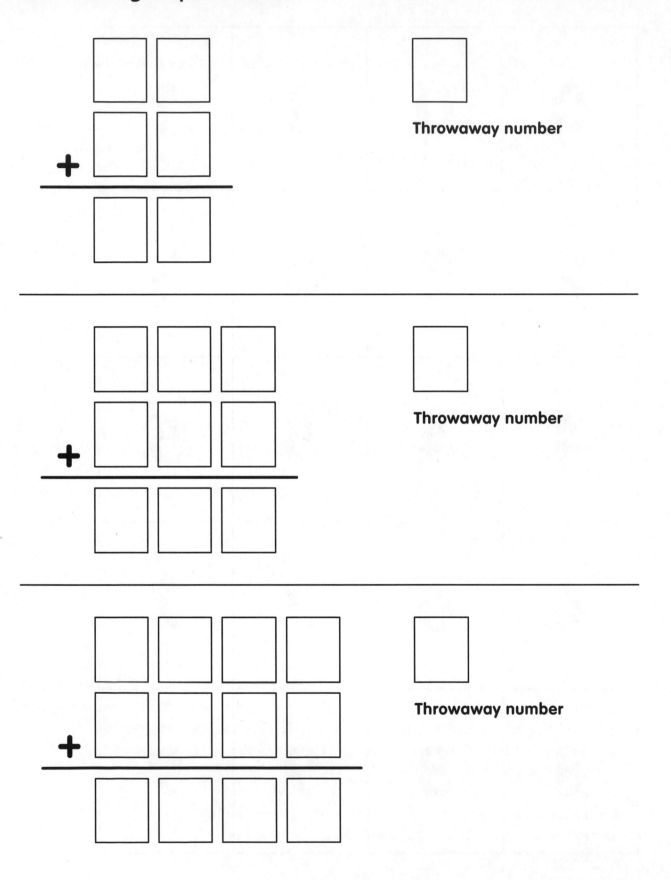

Throwaway number

Throwaway number

Throwaway number

Taking Tokens

Players count and move tokens from among boxes and figure out how many tokens remain in Box #1.

Age Range: 8 to 12
Skill Used: math reasoning
Number of Players: 6
Noise Level: low to moderate
Activity Level: low
Materials: 3 boxes with covers, tokens, response sheet, 6 cards numbered 1 to 6

Setup

Number the boxes 1 through 3, and put a random number of tokens in Box #1. Make a copy of the response sheet for each player.

How to Play

The six numbered cards are placed facedown. Players choose a card to determine which task they are to perform in the round. The numbers correspond with the following tasks:

Player 1—counts and announces how many tokens are in Box #1.
Player 2—moves some of the tokens from Box #1 into Box #2 without looking or counting them out.
Player 3—moves some of the tokens from Box #1 into Box #3 without looking or counting them out.
Player 4—counts and tells how many tokens are in Box #2.
Player 5—counts and tells how many tokens are in Box #3.

Everyone then tries to figure out how many tokens are left in Box #1. When all players have an answer, Player 6 opens Box #1, counts the tokens, and announces the answer. Everyone with the right answer wins that round. Play three more rounds starting with task number selection. The grand champion is the one who wins the most rounds.

Variation

■ Place a unique token in Box #1. Prior to moving any tokens, each player predicts which box that token will be in at the end of the round. After the answer is given at the end of the round, Player 6 will locate the unique token and tell which box it was in. Each player who predicted the correct box earns an extra point.

Tips

■ Prior to play, place tokens in four boxes labeled #1 to speed up the rounds.

■ Use copies of the response sheet provided to help students gather the necessary information and to learn the process/strategy of figuring out Box #1's amount.

Taking Tokens Response Sheets

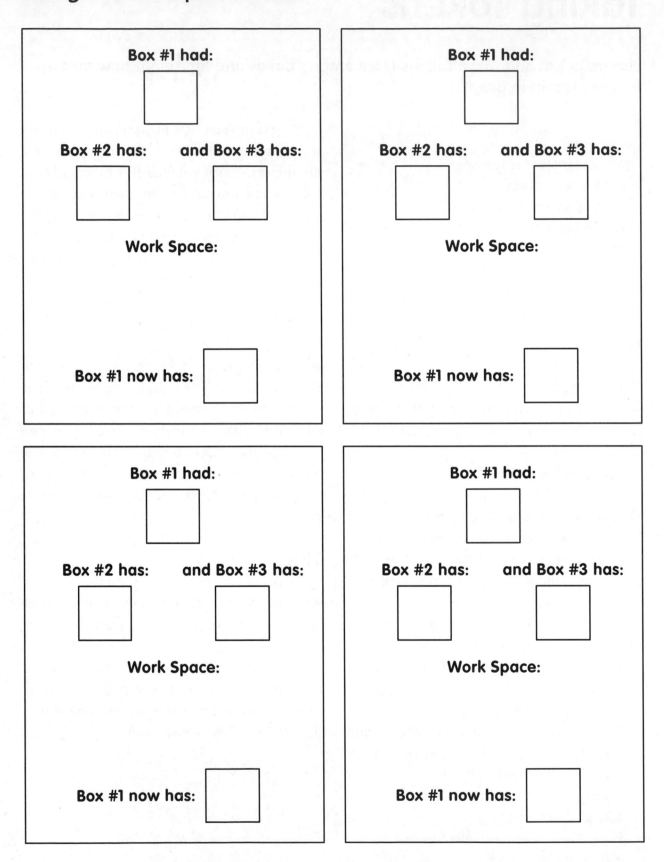

Tic Tac Low

Players write numbers in a grid and add them in different directions to end up with the lowest score.

Age Range: 7 to 8
Skill Used: addition
Number of Players: 2 to 4
Noise Level: low
Activity Level: low
Materials: die, individual Tic Tac Low grids

Setup

Make a copy of the Tic Tac Low grid shown for each player or allow players to draw their own grids.

How to Play

Players take turns rolling a die. The first player writes the number appearing on the roll of the die in any open unshaded spot on his or her Tic Tac Low grid. The die is passed to the next player who rolls and writes that number on his or her grid.

Play continues in the same manner until each player has rolled the die nine times and all of the unshaded squares are filled. Players proceed to cross out any duplicate numbers until only unique numbers are left on each grid. The remaining numbers are added horizontally, vertically, and diagonally. Those sums are added and recorded in the shaded squares. The player with the lowest number is named the winner.

Variation

■ Change the winner to the one having the highest number at the end.

Tic Tac Low Grid

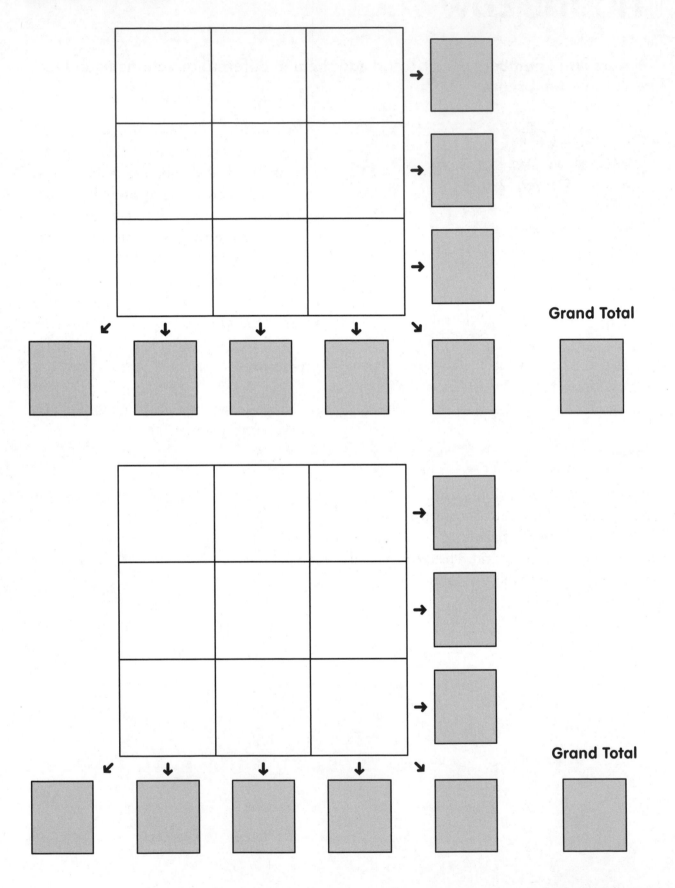

Top Spy

Letters are given numerical values according to a code sheet. Players convert names into code to find their values, trying for the highest score.

Age Range: 7 to 12

Skills Used: addition, understanding of coding, proper noun recognition

Number of Players: 2 to 12

Noise Level: low

Activity Level: low

Materials: letter value chart, pencil and paper

Setup

Using the letter value chart provided, assign a numeric value to each letter of the alphabet. More than one letter can have the same value.

How to Play

To begin, each player writes down five proper nouns of their choice. Players can use their own name, a family member's name, a pet's name, place-name, month, and so on. The code sheet is shown and everyone calculates the value of their five names. The winner is the one having the most points for all five names combined.

Variations

■ After playing this game several times using the first code sheet, give each student an alphabet value chart so he or she can assign values to each letter. Use these for later plays of the game.

■ Challenge players to be the first to find a name in a phone book that will have a certain total.

■ Find proper nouns that are odd, even, one digit, two digits, a square root, and so on.

Tips

■ Be sure to change the values of the letters periodically.

■ If the players are only going to be finding the value of a single word, such as their first name or a type of animal, letter values can be manipulated so even players who often choose short words can end up with the highest total.

Top Spy Letter Value Chart

A		B		C		D		E		F		G		H		I	

J		K		L		M		N		O		P		Q	

R		S		T		U		V		W		X		Y		Z	

What's Shakin'?

Players shake tokens in a special egg carton to score points, which are added together.

Age Range: 7 to 10

Skills Used: knowledge of place value, understanding of expanded notation, addition

Number of Players: 2 to 4

Noise Level: moderate

Activity Level: low

Materials: half-dozen-sized egg carton, tokens, pencil and paper

Setup

This game uses a half-dozen-sized egg carton (2 × 3 section) and nine tokens with the numbers 1 through 9 written on them. One row of three spaces in the carton is labeled with "ones," "tens," and "hundreds." The other row is labeled "out of play." A regular carton can be cut in half, but there should not be a large gap on the cut side.

How to Play

To begin, the first player puts all nine counters in the top of the carton and closes it. The player shakes the carton upside-down to mix the counters and flips it right-side up. Once it is flipped, the shaking is over. When the carton is opened, the position of the counters in the spaces determines the player's score for that round. Empty spaces are assigned a zero and the total value of the counters that fall into the three labeled sections is tallied. For example, if a 2 falls in the "hundreds" section, the "tens" section remains empty and the "ones" section has a 9 and a 3, the total value of the turn is 212. Allow players to use pencil and paper to put the values in expanded notation in order to determine their scores. This would be "200 + 9 + 3" for the example. Players take turns shaking the carton and tallying their scores. After four turns for each player, the cumulative total determines the winner.

Variations

■ Use a whole egg carton and have more place values available. Since the numbers and scores could get far apart, it is helpful to have a "wild" counter in the box and a specially marked section near the middle of the "out of play" half of the carton. If the wild counter falls into this area on a turn, that player can direct any opponent to subtract the amount in the scoring half of the carton while still adding the amount to his or her running total. This rule serves to keep the winning player from getting too far ahead of the others.

■ This game can be played to a target score instead of having a specific number of turns.

Tip

■ Paint the inside of the egg carton to help with the place values. Paint the hundreds place red, tens place blue, and ones place green. Paint the "out of play" spaces black.

Science and Social Studies Games

Egg-streme Matching

Players match state and capital names when they shake an egg carton and have the marked tokens fall into designated spaces.

Age Range: 9 to 12

Skill Used: knowledge of states and capitals

Number of Players: 2 to 4

Noise Level: moderate

Activity Level: low

Materials: egg carton, 50 disk-shaped tokens, game sheet, list of state abbreviations, answer sheet, paper and pencils with erasers

Setup

Randomly paint sections of an egg carton as follows: three green sections, one red section, and two yellow sections. Leave the remaining sections unpainted.

The two-letter abbreviations for each state in the United States should be written in permanent marker on the tokens.

The game sheet needed to play the game shows all the state capital names in alphabetical order with a blank space for the state abbreviation. The list of state abbreviations should be copied and made available to players to determine the name of the state from the abbreviation. The answer key with the correct pairs is also needed to score the game, but this key is not made available as the game is being played.

How to Play

To begin the game, all 50 marked tokens are placed in the lid of the egg carton and the carton is closed. The player chosen to go first shakes the carton and flips it over to allow the counters to fall into the variously colored sections of the container. Once the carton is turned upright, no more shaking should be done and the carton is set down and opened.

The player collects the tokens from the three green sections and records the names of the states they represent next to the corresponding capital names on his or her game sheet in pencil. If the player doesn't know the correct match for the disk, he or she can mark down a guess or choose to skip it. The disks in the red section are collected and these state names are erased from the player's sheet if they were obtained on a previous turn. All of the disks that fall in the yellow spaces are marked on the player's sheet, but they must also be shared with one other player of his or her choice. Once recorded, all the tokens are returned to the carton for the next player's turn.

Play continues to the left with each player shaking the carton and recording his or her matches. The first player to make 25 matches on his or her game sheet is the winner unless an error or incorrect guess is found on the game sheet. In this case, the player is disqualified and play continues until the next person completes 25 matches.

Variations

■ This game can be played until all 50 states have been matched to make it a longer game. An additional green space might be added to the egg carton if this version is used.

■ Other types of matching facts can be adapted to this game format. For younger players, the matches could be uppercase and lowercase letters, for example. For this version of the game, be sure to designate the top and bottom of the letters to avoid confusion with letters such as *d* and *p*.

Tips

■ If it is undesirable to have any mistakes in the game, the answer key to the pairings can be made available to players during the game. This changes the game emphasis to matching rather than memory.

■ Put the state abbreviation and the capital and state sheets on colored paper to easily separate them from the student sheets.

Egg-streme Matching—State Abbreviations

AL	Alabama		MT	Montana
AK	Alaska		NE	Nebraska
AZ	Arizona		NV	Nevada
AR	Arkansas		NH	New Hampshire
CA	California		NJ	New Jersey
CO	Colorado		NM	New Mexico
CT	Connecticut		NY	New York
DE	Delaware		NC	North Carolina
FL	Florida		ND	North Dakota
GA	Georgia		OH	Ohio
HI	Hawaii		OK	Oklahoma
ID	Idaho		OR	Oregon
IL	Illinois		PA	Pennsylvania
IN	Indiana		RI	Rhode Island
IA	Iowa		SC	South Carolina
KS	Kansas		SD	South Dakota
KY	Kentucky		TN	Tennessee
LA	Louisiana		TX	Texas
ME	Maine		UT	Utah
MD	Maryland		VT	Vermont
MA	Massachusetts		VA	Virginia
MI	Michigan		WA	Washington
MN	Minnesota		WV	West Virginia
MS	Mississippi		WI	Wisconsin
MO	Missouri		WY	Wyoming

Egg-streme Matching—Answer Sheet

Albany	NY		Jefferson City	MO
Atlanta	GA		Juneau	AK
Annapolis	MD		Lansing	MI
Augusta	ME		Lincoln	NE
Austin	TX		Little Rock	AR
Baton Rouge	LA		Madison	WI
Bismarck	ND		Montgomery	AL
Boise	ID		Montpelier	VT
Boston	MA		Nashville	TN
Carson City	NV		Oklahoma City	OK
Charleston	WV		Olympia	WA
Cheyenne	WY		Phoenix	AZ
Columbia	SC		Pierre	SD
Columbus	OH		Providence	RI
Concord	NH		Raleigh	NC
Denver	CO		Richmond	VA
Des Moines	IA		Sacramento	CA
Dover	DE		St. Paul	MN
Frankfort	KY		Salem	OR
Harrisburg	PA		Salt Lake City	UT
Hartford	CT		Santa Fe	NM
Helena	MT		Springfield	IL
Honolulu	HI		Tallahassee	FL
Indianapolis	IN		Topeka	KS
Jackson	MS		Trenton	NJ

Egg-streme Matching—Game Sheet

Albany		Jefferson City	
Atlanta		Juneau	
Annapolis		Lansing	
Augusta		Lincoln	
Austin		Little Rock	
Baton Rouge		Madison	
Bismarck		Montgomery	
Boise		Montpelier	
Boston		Nashville	
Carson City		Oklahoma City	
Charleston		Olympia	
Cheyenne		Phoenix	
Columbia		Pierre	
Columbus		Providence	
Concord		Raleigh	
Denver		Richmond	
Des Moines		Sacramento	
Dover		St. Paul	
Frankfort		Salem	
Harrisburg		Salt Lake City	
Hartford		Santa Fe	
Helena		Springfield	
Honolulu		Tallahassee	
Indianapolis		Topeka	
Jackson		Trenton	

Flying Feather Race

Players answer questions to earn the chance to blow their feather down a track to the finish line.

Age Range: 7 to 12
Skill Used: factual knowledge
Number of Players: 2 to 4
Noise Level: moderate
Activity Level: moderate
Materials: feathers of various colors, drinking straws, question-and-answer cards, game board, small pebbles

Setup

This game requires a simple game board in a rectangular shape, as shown in the sample. It should be at least 12 inches wide and 36 inches long, but the exact dimensions are not critical. The board should be divided into 7 to 12 sections across the narrow dimension to mark the race from start to finish. Each section should have a value assigned to it ranging from 1 to 3, with one section near the middle marked "Free." The sections can be numbered randomly in the spaces along the race route. A set of about 50 cards with questions or prompts on one side and answers on the other are needed to play this game. This format facilitates self-checking of answers during the game. The content of the questions can relate to a unit of study, and the game is well suited for use as a review before a test.

How to Play

Each player chooses a feather and a straw to use for the entire game. Because the size and shape of the feathers and straws can sometimes affect the outcome of the game, players cannot exchange their game pieces once selected. Sharing or exchanging straws is also prohibited for hygienic reasons.

To begin, each feather is placed behind the starting line with a pebble to anchor it down. Pebbles are used throughout the game to keep feathers from moving between plays. The player chosen to go first selects the top card and answers the question. If the answer is correct, the player removes the pebble and is allowed one puff of air through the straw to move his or her own feather along the game board. Once the feather settles, it is anchored again with a pebble. Players take turns drawing cards and answering questions for the first round.

For the second round, each player must correctly answer the number of questions indicated by the space that his or her feather is resting upon. If the feather is on a line, then the smaller number is used for the turn. If the player answers all of the questions correctly, that player receives a chance to blow his or her feather. If any one of the group of questions is missed, the player loses that turn. Landing on the "Free" space means that the player can blow into the straw to advance his or her feather without having to answer a question at all.

The first player to advance his or her feather across the finish line is the winner. If a player accidentally blows his or her feather off the side of the board during a turn, that player must return to the starting line. In the unlikely event that a player blows an opponent's feather off the board during a play, the opponent's feather is put back in its original position and the player blowing it off must go back to the starting line.

Variation

■ An extra-large version of this game can be played using an outdoor play area marked in chalk. Instead of feathers and straws, players can mark their spaces by actually standing in them. To advance, players can use a balloon, blowing it up and releasing it to let the escaping air send the balloon on. The unpredictability of the balloon's direction is a big part of the fun. Only one question card per turn is needed to make this game interesting and move it along, so no numbers are needed on the play space.

Tips

■ The position of the player blowing a feather should be agreed upon before the start of play. The length of the board can dictate this and home rules should be in place. Generally, a player should stand or sit behind the starting line or at the side of the game board. No part of the player's body or straw should touch the board during the game.

■ Beware of playing this game near open windows, air vents, or ceiling fans. A calm corner is best.

Flying Feather Race Game Board

(Make an enlarged copy for game.)

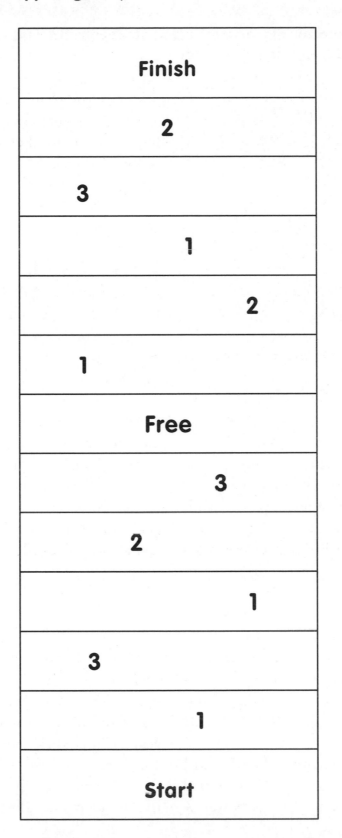

Finish
2
3
1
2
1
Free
3
2
1
3
1
Start

Geographic Name Chain

Players search a map for place-names that start with the last letter of the place-name that came before.

Age Range: 9 to 12

Skill Used: reading, map reading

Number of Players: 2 to 4

Noise Level: low

Activity Level: low

Materials: atlas or several maps, stopwatch, paper and pencil

Setup

Have an atlas or set of maps available for play.

How to Play

Players choose one map in an atlas by opening to a random page or by choosing one of the maps provided. The first player points to any name on the map, reads it to the group, and writes it down. This player uses the stopwatch to time the others. The paper is passed to the next player who must find another name on the map that begins with the last letter of the name just written. The player must point to the next name within one minute and then writes the name on the paper next to the previous word. For example, "Canberra—Australia—Adelaide" might be written for a map of Australia.

If no suitable place-name is found before time runs out or an error is made, the round ends with the elimination of that player. A round is completed when only one player remains. A point is awarded to the player who found the last word of a round, and the play continues to a predetermined total to determine a winner.

Variations

■ A more competitive game can be done with individuals writing their chains during a set time limit. At the end of the time, compare the length of the chains, with players with the longest chains earning points toward a winning total.

■ Use detailed diagrams to find chains. Examples are a cross section of a ship or the parts of a horse. Players will be encouraged to study the diagram in detail and notice more obscure parts in an attempt to make long chains of terms or find "stumpers" that will end a chain, depending on which version of the game is being played.

Tip

■ Make a "Chain Hall of Fame" by keeping track of the longest chain made with each map. A cooperative version of this game can be played in which a team tries to make the longest chain possible from a certain map. The total can be recorded, and other teams can try to find a longer chain and put their result in the top slot in the "Chain Hall of Fame."

Geography Baseball

Players find locations in an atlas when the name of the place is "pitched" to them. Successful "hitters" advance around the bases to score for their team.

> **Age Range:** 10 to 12
> **Skill Used:** map reading
> **Number of Players:** 8 to 10
> **Noise Level:** moderate
> **Activity Level:** moderate
> **Materials:** atlas, cards with target locations printed on them, a small baseball diamond game board and tokens (optional), die, timer

Setup

Fifty or more cards are prepared with names of locations that appear in the atlas index and clearly on the maps. For example the cards could read: "Find the country of Yap," "Locate the Yellow River," "Point to the Erie Canal," and so on. Choose names of features that are familiar to the players.

How to Play

Two equal teams of players should arrange themselves in a "batting order" according to alphabetical order or some other arbitrary means. Four locations in the room are designated as bases and space is cleared for players to move between them. The starting team is chosen by a coin flip or any common random method and gathers at home plate with the atlas.

The starting team gives the atlas to the first batter who rolls the die to determine whether the question will represent a single—1, double—2, triple—3, or home run—4, as shown on the key. A roll of 5 is a foul and the batter rolls again. A roll of 6 is a strike and the batter rolls again, unless it is the third strike.

Once the value of the question is determined, the first person on the pitching team reads the first card, which is a place-name found in the atlas. The timer is set for two minutes when the item is read to the batter. The batter uses any desired method to locate the place in the atlas and points to it, saying, "Here it is." If the answer is correct and within the time limit, the batter moves the designated number of bases in the room and the other players on base advance as well. A point is scored for the team when a player crosses home plate.

If the answer is wrong or not found within the time limit, the batter is out and moves to the back of the batting order. Players on base do not advance but stay on base until the team reaches three outs and the teams exchange places. Play continues until a predetermined number of innings have been played. The team with the most runs scored wins the game.

Variations

■ Make this a dictionary game or an encyclopedia game by providing a different reference book and a related set of cards.

■ For a quieter game with a lower activity level, make a game board with a baseball diamond. Players can use tokens to show their progress around the bases.

Tips

■ The time limit can be adjusted depending on the skill of the players and the complexity of the reference book used. Two minutes is a suggestion, but it might be frustrating for some. A bonus base could be given for finding the item in two minutes, and the regular number of bases for a longer time limit.

■ Add an umpire to the game to settle disputes about timing or a roll of the die. This person can also make sure that players move the correct number of bases and that the score is recorded correctly.

■ Older students can prepare sets of cards to be used when the game is played at a later time.

Geography Baseball Key

1	Single
2	Double
3	Triple
4	Home Run
5	Foul
6	Strike

Geography Baseball Game Board

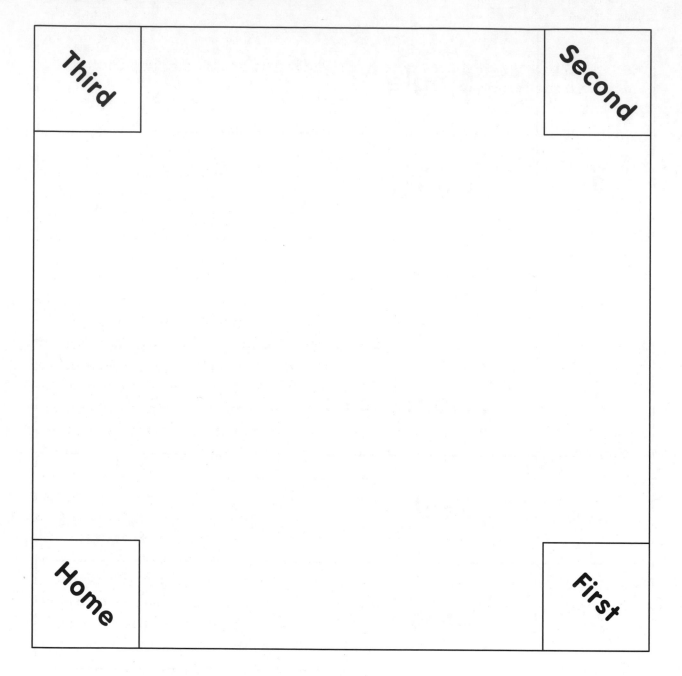

Land on It

Players toss their game pieces onto a particular grid square and use coordinates to tell the locations.

> **Age Range:** 7 to 9
> **Skill Used:** knowledge of map coordinates
> **Number of Players:** 4
> **Noise Level:** moderate to high
> **Activity Level:** moderate to high
> **Materials:** 6′3″ × 6′3″ grid, 4 beanbags or small stuffed animals, masking tape

Setup

Make a 6′3″ × 6′3″ mat out of large paper, tarp, or canvas. As shown, draw a line 3 inches in from the left and the bottom. Divide the rest of the space into six equal columns and rows. In the 3-inch column, write letters from *A* to *F*. In the 3-inch row, write numbers from 1 to 6, as shown in the sample.

In the grid spaces, draw pictures or write words that go with a particular topic or unit the class is learning about, such as geometric shapes, math symbols, state or country capitals, and so on. Place the mat on the floor and use masking tape to designate a throwing line 6 feet away.

How to Play

Each player selects a beanbag or small animal as a game piece. Players take turns naming an item on the grid. Standing at a line about 6 feet from the grid, players toss their game pieces at the same time, trying to make them land in the correct spot. Each player whose game piece lands on the correct spot says the coordinates of the location. Each player who says the correct coordinates earns a point.

Players retrieve their game pieces and get ready to toss the game pieces again when the next player names an item on the grid. The players with the most points at the end win.

Variation

■ Have players practice using descriptions or adjectives by drawing pictures of objects with distinct physical characteristics on the game board. Play as previously described but in addition to telling the coordinates, each player landing on the square also has to use different descriptive words for the item. Suppose, for example, a mouse is one of the pictures. The first player landing on the mouse might say, "The gray mouse is in space C, 2." The second player might say, "The tiny mouse is in space C, 2."

Tips

. . . .

■ For older players, make the spaces smaller so more throwing accuracy is necessary.

■ Wait for all players who landed on the described space to tell their answers. Then tell or confirm the correct answer.

■ Make a set of cards with the pictures or words that match the items on the mat's grids. Include the coordinates for each on the card for easier checking. Use the cards to direct the tossing.

Land on It Grid

(Make an enlarged copy of this grid for game.)

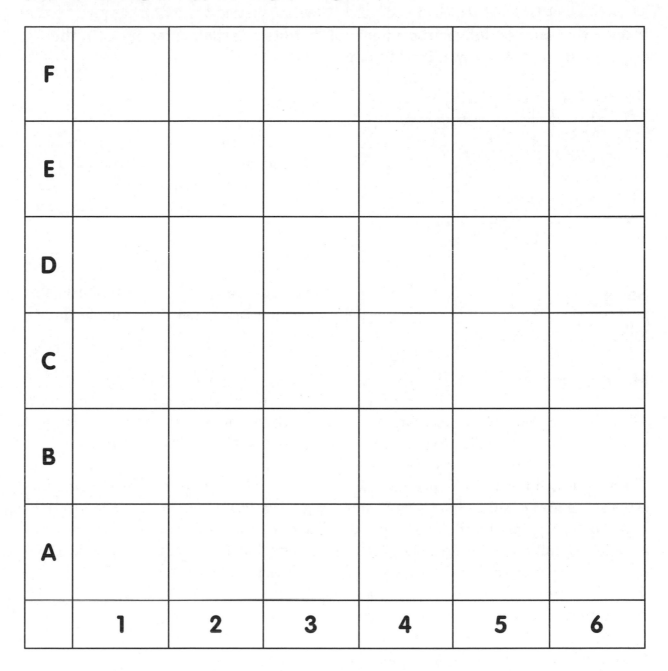

Name an Animal

Players who successfully name an animal that fits a certain category earn the opportunity to toss a toy animal to other players.

Age Range: 7 to 10
Skill Used: categorizing
Number of Players: 7 to 14
Noise Level: moderate
Activity Level: moderate
Materials: beanbag toy animal

Setup

None needed.

How to Play

All of the players stand in a circle. One player is selected to be "It." This player stands in the center of the circle with the toy animal. The toy is tossed to one of the players in the circle as the player in the center says an animal group (e.g., mammal, insect, reptile, amphibian, bird, fish, or invertebrate). Group names should be selected with awareness of the players' levels of knowledge. The player who catches the toy must then name a specific animal that goes with that group and toss the animal back to the thrower before the thrower counts to 10. No animal name can be repeated. If the last player can name a correct animal, he or she trades places with the thrower and the game continues in the same manner.

Variation

■ Play the game in the same manner substituting states, capitals, countries, and continents for the categories. Use an inflatable globe rather than a toy animal for this game.

Tips

■ A large pom-pom can be tossed in this game. It is easy to catch and can't be thrown too hard.

■ Encourage players who become "It" to make sure everyone has had an opportunity to catch the toy and answer before tossing it to players who already had a chance.

■ Establish a rhythm or procedure for counting to 10. Players might decide to say "and" between each number or some other word so it doesn't become a race to see who can count the fastest.

On the Level

Players answer questions to collect randomly sized blocks of wood to stack in two piles. The challenge is to make level stacks of the greatest height.

Age Range: 8 to 12

Skills Used: factual knowledge, strategic thinking, measurement of height

Number of Players: 4 to 7

Noise Level: moderate

Activity Level: moderate

Materials: 30 wooden blocks of various thicknesses, level, ruler, numbered question sheet with an answer key, bag

Setup

A set of numbered questions and answers are written on a sheet of paper. Questions do not have to be in any particular order but should relate to a particular subject area.

Game pieces are flat blocks of wood in various thicknesses that can be stacked easily. It is important that the pieces be random, rather than uniform in shape and size. Each piece should be numbered to correspond with a question on the answer key. An additional three pieces should be marked as "Free." Before starting, all the wooden pieces are placed in the bag.

How to Play

Players are divided into three teams (or individuals), plus one game director to read questions. The first player reaches into the bag and pulls out a wooden piece. The game director reads the question matching the number on the block. If the player answers correctly, the block is kept. If the answer is wrong, it is put back in the bag and the correct answer is not revealed.

Each player or team collects blocks in this way and strategically places them in two stacks as they are accumulated to keep the stacks level with one another. Once placed in a stack, a block cannot be moved to the other tower nor can blocks be exchanged between towers.

Play continues until all questions have been answered correctly and all the blocks have been collected and stacked. The game director uses the level and ruler to check the evenness and height of the stacks. The winner is the player (or team) with two stacks that are closest to being level. Second place goes to the player with the highest stack.

Variations

■ The numbered questions can be math facts, states and capitals, words to rhyme, vocabulary definitions, or any category of information to be practiced by the players.

■ Three sets of related questions can be used to play three rounds of this game. In this version of the game, level stacks score two points and the tallest stack scores one point. The player or team with the most points at the end of three rounds is the winner.

Tips

■ The blocks can be easily made out of balsa wood, which is available in craft stores. Different thicknesses are available, and balsa wood requires little sanding. As an alternative, slices of stock lumber could be used for the blocks.

■ Carpenters, contractors, or home-building centers are good sources of wood scraps for this game. These scraps might require more sanding, but the resulting pieces would be harder to stack into even towers and more random pieces tend to make the game more interesting.

Team Towers

Teams earn toothpicks and marshmallows by answering questions and then compete to construct the tallest tower.

Age Range: 5 to 12

Skill Used: factual knowledge

Number of Players: 5 to 11

Noise Level: moderate

Activity Level: moderate

Materials: question-and-answer cards, toothpicks, mini-marshmallows, timer, ruler

Setup

Question cards are prepared using vocabulary words, facts, and concepts from a particular unit of study, and the answers are included on the reverse to make them self-checking for players. For example, if the topic was about world exploration, a sample question could be: Name the monarch who financed Columbus's first voyage (Queen Isabella of Spain). There should be about 10 cards per player. Marshmallows should be tested to ensure that they are neither stuck together nor hard. Fresh marshmallows work best for this game.

How to Play

One player is chosen as the game director and the others form teams of two. The game director reads a question to the player selected to go first. If the player responds correctly, he or she takes the card. Cards are shown to each player in turn until all the cards have been collected. Then, the players "buy" building sup-plies from the game director by exchanging cards. One card buys a toothpick; two cards buy one marshmallow.

When all teams have traded for building supplies, the game director starts the timer and teams compete to build the tallest tower possible with their supplies within five min-utes. Once building starts, supplies cannot be traded or exchanged. When time is up, the tower must stand on its own. Any team attempting to topple another tower by blow-ing on it or rocking the table is disqualified. At the end of the time limit, structures are measured by the game director and the team with the tallest tower is the winner.

Variation

■ Popcorn and pieces of uncooked spaghetti can be substituted for the marshmallows and toothpicks. Using uncooked spaghetti adds a new twist to the game because the pieces will not all be the exact same size. They can be "priced" by length at 3 inches per card. The spaghetti version of the game also allows players to break the pieces to improve their structures.

Tip

■ It is wise to set guidelines for disposal of the building supplies at the end of the game. Players will probably want to eat the marsh-mallows or popcorn (if used) once the winner is selected.

Volcano

Red tokens are added to a cup each time a question is answered. The last player to put in a token before the cup overflows, or "erupts," is the winner.

Age Range: 7 to 12
Skill Used: factual knowledge
Number of Players: 2 to 5
Noise Level: moderate
Activity Level: low
Materials: small paper cup, question-and-answer cards, 70 red tokens, die

Setup

Preparation for this game requires gathering the needed materials and writing question cards. There should be about eight cards for each player participating. Any set of questions relating to a unit of study can appear on the cards with the answers on the back. The format of the game lends itself to earth science questions, but it is not limited to these. A sample question for "Volcano" could be: What is the term for the huge pieces of Earth's crust that move slowly on top of Earth's mantle? (Tectonic plates.) The paper cup and tokens can be of any convenient size, but the cup should hold only about 50 tokens before overflowing. Use of red tokens is suggested to simulate molten lava.

How to Play

Players take turns answering the question on the top question card. When the answer is correct, the player rolls the die and puts that number of red tokens in the paper cup using only one hand. Play continues with players taking turns answering questions and adding tokens to the cup. Players try to avoid having their turns cause an overflow of tokens, or an eruption. When that happens, the last player to have successfully added to the cup is the winner.

Any player can cause an "earthquake" in the volcano by shaking down the cup. This can make more space for tokens, but can also result in an overflow. A player who does this takes the chance of losing by causing an eruption that ends the game. If more space is successfully created in this way, however, play continues.

Tips

■ Use red beans, red-dyed pasta shells, red marbles, or red cubes in place of the tokens.

■ A more realistic volcano made of painted salt dough can make the game more fun to play as long as the crater is the right size for the tokens used.

■ If only two players are playing, the cup can be partly filled before starting the game.

Wait to Weigh In

Players collect pebbles in an attempt to have the heaviest set of items.

> **Age Range:** 7 to 10
> **Skills Used:** factual knowledge, measuring weight
> **Number of Players:** 3 to 5
> **Noise Level:** moderate
> **Activity Level:** low
> **Materials:** 60 small pebbles, a kitchen scale, question-and-answer cards

Setup

The pebbles should be weighed to make sure that each one weighs between 0 and 2 ounces. The scale should read clearly in ounces for this game. There should be enough self-checking question-and-answer cards for each player to have 10 turns, but no more than the total number of pebbles.

How to Play

The cards are shuffled and placed in a stack within easy reach of all players. Players take turns drawing a card and answering the questions. A player keeps the card if he or she answers correctly but discards it if the answer is incorrect. Each player takes 10 turns to collect a maximum of 10 cards.

The player with the fewest cards gets the first chance to choose one item. The player with the second fewest cards chooses next and so on, keeping the same order of choosing until all the cards have been exchanged for items. Each player puts all of his or her pebbles on the scale at once and records the combined weight. The player with the highest recorded weight wins the game.

Tips

■ The box of pebbles can be closed for the question portion of the game if it seems to distract the players.

■ Players should not handle items before choosing them. The rule can be to take any item you touch.

■ Add "mystery items" such as small boxes or bits of fabric holding unknown contents. There should be at least one such item per player if these are used.

Where Will You Land?

Players move their tokens around a game board using compass directions and collect prizes along the way.

Age Range: 8 to 10

Skill Used: understanding of map coordinates and compass directions

Number of Players: 2 to 4

Noise Level: low to moderate

Activity Level: low

Materials: die, blank cube for direction die, game piece for each player, game board, stickers or pictures

Setup

Prepare the direction die by labeling a blank cube with N, S, E, W, and your choice of repeating two directions or adding consequences such as "Roll again," "Lose turn," or "Choose a space." Make a game board with an 11 × 11 grid as shown. Place an X in the middle. Draw or cut out pictures that fit in the game board's squares.

How to Play

Choose one player to be the cartographer, who randomly places the pictures in spaces on the game board. All of the players begin play from the X in the middle of the board.

Players take turns rolling both dice and moving their game pieces the correct number of spaces in the direction shown on the direction die. The game piece stays in that space until the player's next turn. If a player lands on a space with a picture, the player takes it. If the roll takes the player off the game board, the playing piece is returned to the X for that player's next turn. The winner is the player who collects the most pictures.

Variation

■ Make several game boards with the X placed in various positions.

Tips

■ Make a pocket or place an envelope on the back of the game board to store the pictures.

■ Use computer art in each square to create your pictures for the game.

■ Decorate the game board with pictures to set a theme. These pictures could include endangered animals, landmarks, states, space objects, treasure, and so on.

Where Will You Land? Game Board

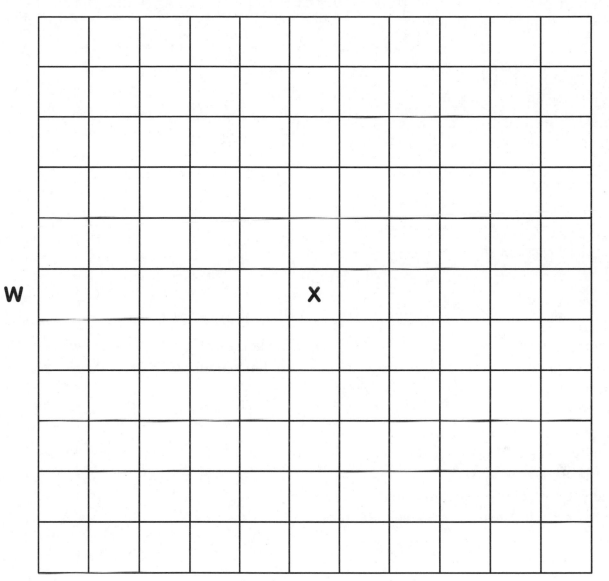

Strategy and Memory Games

Bed of Nails

Players put rubber bands on an array of nails following rules about which nails can be encircled.

Age Range: 7 to 10

Skill Used: strategic thinking

Number of Players: 3

Noise Level: moderate

Activity Level: moderate

Materials: rubber bands in three colors, wooden game board, 100 nails, pair of dice

Setup

The game board is a 12″ × 12″ piece of wood. It is prepared by pounding nails into the board in a half-inch grid pattern, with the heads of the nails sticking up about an inch. The points of the nails should not protrude from the bottom of the board. The grid should be 10 by 10 nails. The rubber bands should be sorted into the three colors. About 30 of each color are needed. Thin bands of about 1 or 2 inches in diameter are easier to use for this game since they do not need to be doubled to make a play stay in place.

How to Play

Each player chooses rubber bands of one color to use for the game and has these in a pile. For the first round, each player rolls only one die. The number rolled determines the number of nails to enclose with the band, except for a roll of 1, which stands for 7 in this entire game.

Once each player has placed his or her first band on the board, players take turns rolling the pair of dice for their turns. When they roll, the larger number showing (with 1 still equaling 7) indicates the total number of nails to have within their shape. The smaller number tells how many nails to include that are already within another shape. For example, a roll showing a 1 and a 4 means that the player must enclose a total of seven nails in his or her shape and four of the seven must be already enclosed in another shape on the board. A roll showing a 4 and a 2 would require the player to enclose four nails, with two of the four already within another band. There is no limit to how many times the same nail can be used in a play.

If a player rolls doubles, he or she loses a turn. If there is no space available to play their roll, players must pass. The winner is the last one who is able to make a play on the board. This will happen when the supply of available unused nails is running low and players have to pass for a complete round.

Giant Cube

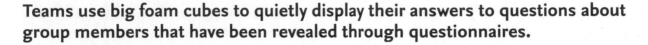

Teams use big foam cubes to quietly display their answers to questions about group members that have been revealed through questionnaires.

Age Range: 9 to 12
Skills Used: listening, memory
Number of Players: 7 to 21
Noise Level: moderate
Activity Level: moderate
Materials: questionnaires, two or more foam cubes measuring 6 to 10 inches on a side, chalkboard or large paper to post scores

Setup

Players for this game should be part of a group that has had some experience playing and working together for at least a few days. During this time, players should fill in their own questionnaires and have the opportunity to share their answers with the group in a casual setting.

The information used for the game is drawn from the questionnaire data and involves personal preferences including, but not limited to, favorite color, pets, favorite subject, special talents, hobbies, interesting trips taken, and collections. The players' answers on the questionnaires should be scanned for interesting data to become game questions. The questions for the game must either have a yes or no answer or four choices labeled A, B, C, and D. These six answers are written on the faces of the giant cubes.

A complete set of questions is created for each specific group of players with the correct answer listed. Some examples include:

1. Sherrie's favorite animal is the turtle. (yes)
2. Jim, Donna, and Chris have something in common:
   A. They have no pets.
   B. They all like blue.
   C. They play the piano.
   D. Math is their favorite subject.

How to Play

One game director is selected to read the questions from the questionnaires and keep the score. The rest of the players are divided into at least two equal teams. Teams need to form huddles so that they can discuss answers without the other teams overhearing them. These huddles should be side by side along a line facing the game director. The arrangement is similar to the start of a relay race.

The game director reads the questions and the team members confer to choose the best answer. One member of the team holds the cube to show the team's answer on the side toward the game director. When all teams have positioned their cubes, the game director announces the correct answer and posts one point for each team with that choice showing. Questioning continues with teams sharing the responsibility of holding the cube for the answer.

When a set number of questions have been given, the team with the most points is the winner.

Variations

■ This game can be used as a practice session for any set of content area questions. The team approach makes it a good way to bring about some valuable discussion about the information.

■ When there are more than two teams to begin with, this game can be played in rounds with the lowest team being eliminated the first time. Then the remaining teams can answer another set of questions until only one team remains.

Tip

■ The questions can be prepared on overhead transparencies, or in a PowerPoint presentation, and projected onto a screen so that players can read them as they deliberate.

Giant Cube Sample Questionnaire

What is your name? _____

_____

Do you have a nickname? _____ What is it? _____

_____

What are your hobbies? _____

_____

Do you have any pets? _____ What kind? _____
What are their names? _____

Can you swim? _____

_____

Can you ride a bike? _____

_____

Do you play an instrument? _____ Which one(s)? _____

_____

What is the most exciting thing you have ever done? _____

_____

What is the scariest thing that ever happened to you? _____

_____

What is an unusual thing about you? _____

_____

What is your favorite color? _____

_____

What is your favorite subject? _____

_____

Hen and Chicks

A "hen" tries to find the missing "chicks" by listening to them peep.

Age Range: 4 to 6
Skill Used: listening
Number of Players: 6 to 15
Noise Level: moderate to high
Activity Level: moderate
Materials: die

Setup

None needed.

How to Play

All of the players need to be sitting at tables or desks. One player, who becomes the hen, is selected to leave the room. One of the players remaining in the room rolls a die and taps that number of players who become peeping chicks. The chicks and the remaining players put their heads down so their mouths are hidden; they don't have to hide their eyes.

The player who rolled the die and chose the chicks invites the hen back into the room. When the hen clucks, the chicks peep. The hen tries to find the chicks by tapping them on the shoulder. If the player who is tapped is a chick, the chick, who no longer peeps, follows the hen around as the search for the other chicks continues.

If the game is to be played again, choose the next hen from the group of players who weren't chicks.

Variation

■ Blindfold the hen who stands in front of the room. The hen tries to identify the chicks by calling names as they peep.

Tip

■ Be sure all players know how to cluck and peep.

Junk Drawer

Players put miscellaneous household objects into groups using their own sorting rules.

Age Range: 6 to 9
Skill Used: categorizing
Number of Players: 4
Noise Level: moderate
Activity Level: low
Materials: box of miscellaneous items that might be found in a junk drawer, die, timer, string

Setup

The miscellaneous items collected can be placed in a single box for this game. Six 20-inch pieces of string should be tied into circles.

How to Play

The game is played with two teams of two. The starting team rolls the die to determine how many groupings to make using all of the items in the box. A roll of 1 allows the team to decide for themselves how many groupings to make. They must have at least two groups of things but no more than six. The other team sets the timer for three minutes, and then the sorters begin placing objects in groups surrounded by the circles of string. Remind players that the circles need not be perfect, but simply enclose the desired objects.

At the end of the time limit, the sorting team stops. The sorting team explains their sorting rules and earns one point for every group they made that follows their stated rule. For example, one group of things might be called "office supplies" and would score a point as long as all of the items included are indeed office supplies. A two-point penalty would be assessed if the team failed to make as many groupings as indicated by the roll of the die. A "miscellaneous" group is permitted on each turn if players have difficulty making enough true categories to complete their turn, but it will not score a point.

The objects are returned to the box, and the other team rolls the die and sorts the objects. Teams may not repeat the use of a sorting rule except for the "miscellaneous" group if desired. Each team sorts the box of items three times, and the team with the highest score wins.

Items for this game can include, but are not limited to, the following ideas:

Buttons
Paper clips (varied colors and sizes)
Small toys (tops, animals, cars, blocks, etc.)
Pencils
Keys
Tape measure
Flashlight
Eraser
Feather
Rubber bands (different colors and sizes)
Toothpicks
Ribbon
Shells

Pebbles
Photos
Coupons
Doll accessories
Nails and screws
Springs
Beads
Thread
Safety pins
Coins

Variations

■ More advanced players can overlap two strings to make a Venn diagram. The items in the shared section would score as an additional point. If a team is able to make a correct sort using three overlapping circles, it can be an instant win.

■ Provide containers of just one type of item so players have to observe and determine specific attributes when making their groups. For example: plastic bread tags can be grouped by color, size, shape of the hole, and numbers on the tag; keys can be grouped by type of metal, size, identifying marks/words, shape of the bow or top of the key, whether the stem is ground on one side or two; pencils can be grouped by color, size, type, number of sides, graphics; and so on.

■ Teams can use different sets of items and challenge the other teams to explain their sorting rule. If a team can stump all the others, they win.

Tips

■ The contents of the box can literally be gathered from a junk drawer for this game.

■ Avoid including dangerous items such as matchbooks, pocket knives, or lighters.

■ Avoid items such as batteries or permanent markers for younger players.

Now You See It, Now You Don't 🧠

Players observe a number of objects and then try to identify ones secretly removed.

Age Range: 4 to 12

Skill Used: memory

Number of Players: 2

Noise Level: low

Activity Level: low

Materials: tray or large shallow box, 20 or more small common items, a piece of paper or fabric large enough to cover the tray or box, stopwatch or one-minute timer

Setup

Collect 20 or more small, common items.

How to Play

The first player secretly chooses 10 of the small items and arranges them on the tray or in the box so they aren't touching each other while the second player is turned away from the area of play. The paper or fabric cover is carefully placed over the chosen items. When the second player turns around, the cover is removed. That player has one minute to look at all of the items. Then the cover is replaced and the player turns away again. The first player secretively removes the cover and two of the items. The second player turns around and is given one minute to identify the items that were removed. If the items can be identified, that player is the winner. If the items can't be identified, the first player is the winner.

Variations

■ Place vocabulary words, math flash cards, or similar groups of items on the tray or in the box rather than the small items.

■ The first player puts the 10 items in a cloth bag. Without looking, the second player feels them and/or counts them. The first player removes some items. The second player feels again and tells either how many items were removed or which items were removed.

Tip

■ Adjust the number of items initially placed on the tray for the age level of the players.

Pirate Loot

A "pirate" arranges treasure on a checkerboard and allows the "mates" to look at it for a minute. Points are collected for remembering where the loot was hidden.

Age Range: 6 to 10

Skill Used: memory

Number of Players: 2 to 6

Noise Level: moderate

Activity Level: low

Materials: checkerboard, timer, scarf, game sheet with blank checkerboard, small objects or pictures to place on checkerboard squares, pencils, ship token

Setup

This game uses small pictures or objects that depict pirate treasure or supplies. (See the list of suggestions in the How to Play section.) Three-dimensional objects make the game more appealing, but small laminated pictures can be used if objects are not readily at hand. Each item should fit on a checkerboard square with the exception of a ship token, which should cover two squares. Make copies of the game sheet for every player.

How to Play

One player is chosen to be the pirate. All the other players turn away from the board while the pirate takes all the items, including the ship token and puts them randomly on the checkerboard. When the pirate is done "hiding the loot," the board is covered with a scarf.

Once covered, the pirate says "Ahoy, mates!" and the others turn back to face the board.

A timer is set for one minute and the pirate reveals the board for all to see. Players use the time to quietly study the board, but may not make written notes. At the end of the time limit, the scarf is put back over the board. Then, players use the blank checkerboard game sheet and mark an X on each square ("X marks the spot") that matches an item's location on the pirate's board. The spaces occupied by the ship token should be labeled with the word *ship*.

When all players have finished marking their game sheets, the scarf is removed again and the answers are checked. Players get one point for each location correctly marked and five points for knowing the ship's location. Points are recorded. Each player gets a turn being the pirate and hiding the items. Points for all the rounds are tallied to determine the winner. The player with the most points wins the game.

The following items or pictures could be used as game pieces:

Gold earring
Pearls
Spanish coin replicas
Plastic gems (various colors)
Cocktail sword
Treasure chest
Silver or gold ingot

Cannon
Cannonball
Map
Telescope
Ship's wheel
Pirate's eye patch
Anchor
Message in a bottle
Pirate flag

Variations

■ Let the pirate decide how many items to place on the board.

■ Players can earn double points by drawing or writing the name of the item in the right locations.

Tips

■ The record sheets can be color copies of a checkerboard to make the game a bit easier. Players then have the advantage of remembering locations using the red and black color cues as well as location.

■ Have a pirate hat, eye patch, or scarf for the pirate to wear.

Pirate Loot Game Sheet

Write Xs to mark the spots where the pirate hid the loot.

Write "Ship" in the spaces where the ship was located.

Scores:

Taking a Trip

Players take turns adding items to a list of things being taken on a trip, while trying to remember all the items that came before.

Age Range: 7 to 12
Skill Used: categorizing, memory
Number of Players: 4 to 20
Noise Level: moderate
Activity Level: low to moderate
Materials: travel bag cards

Setup

Copy several travel bag cards or draw cards with suitcases, backpacks, or bags. Write a theme or topic on the back of each traveling bag card. Topics might include items needed for going to the beach; animals to collect for a zoo; shopping in a grocery store; the name of a state, country, or continent; or an initial consonant or consonant blend.

How to Play

The first player draws a travel bag card and reads it to the other players. That player starts the game by saying, "I'm taking a trip and I'm going to take/pack/collect (whatever is appropriate to the theme card) _____." The player then names an item related to the topic. The travel bag card is passed to the next player who repeats the entire list of things said and then adds an item of his or her own. Players cannot repeat items that have already been listed. Continue play in this manner until time is up.

Variations

■ Require that a number and/or an adjective be said with each specific item.

■ The first item mentioned is written on the board. The next item said has to start with the initial letter, second item with the next letter, and so on until the word is done. Start over with the next stated word.

■ Name the state and capital or the capital and country for where players are going.

Tips

■ Let players act out their items to help players as they are repeating the list.

■ See if anyone can remember the list after lunch, the next morning, and so on.

■ Be sure to congratulate everyone for working so hard to remember the list.

Taking a Trip Cards

Tricky Triangles

Players connect dots to try to form the most triangles.

Age Range: 7 to 12
Skill Used: strategic thinking
Number of Players: 2
Noise Level: low to moderate
Activity Level: low
Materials: pencil and paper

Setup

None needed.

How to Play

One player draws between 20 to 40 dots randomly on a sheet of paper. The other player starts by connecting two of the dots with a line. The first player connects another two dots with a line. Play continues back and forth with the players drawing lines to form a triangle having no dot inside and not touching any other triangle. When a triangle is formed, that player writes his or her initials in it to claim it. Play ends when no more triangles can be made. Each player counts the triangles he or she completed, and the one who made the most triangles wins.

What's My Name?

Players are challenged to remember each other's animal code name in order to collect number cards and win the game.

Age Range: 6 to 10

Skill Used: number matching, memory

Number of Players: 4 to 6

Noise Level: moderate

Activity Level: low

Materials: paper or cardstock to make numbered card decks

Setup

Prepare two decks of cards for this game, using the sample cards provided. On one color paper make a 40-card deck numbered 1 to 10, four times. Make the other 10-card deck numbered 1 to 10, using paper of a different color.

How to Play

The game begins with the players sitting in a circle. Each player chooses a number card from the 10-card deck and reveals the card by placing it in front of him or her. As the player does that, he or she names an animal, which becomes that player's code name. No other player may repeat an animal name. The shuffled pack of 40 cards is placed facedown in the center. Players take turns flipping one card at a time and placing it faceup on a pile next to the deck. If the card flipped matches another person's card, the player who flipped the card has to correctly say that person's animal name to win all of the cards in the pile. Some numbers will not have an animal name because the game is played with fewer than 10 players. Play ends when the original pile is used up. The person with the most cards wins.

Variation

■ Use other categories for the player's names such as places, kitchen utensils, things in a refrigerator, types of cars, indoor hobbies, or wildflowers.

What's My Name? Number Cards

(Make four copies of this card in one color and one copy in another color.)

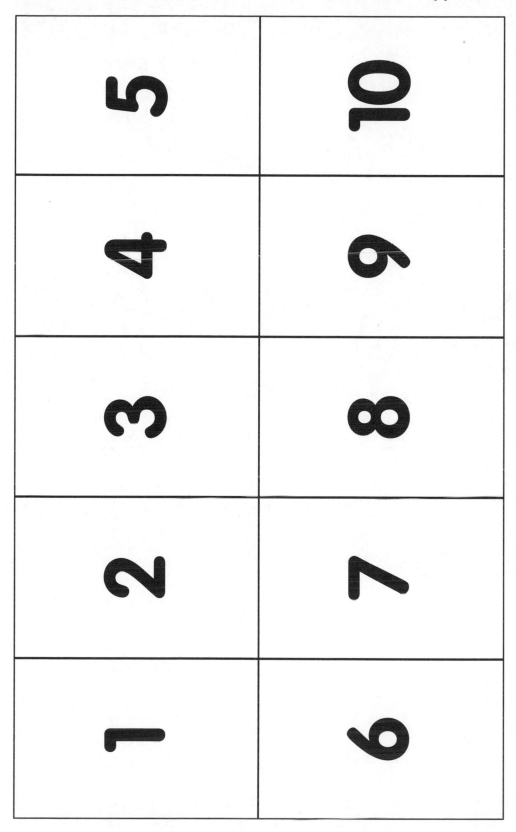

Who's First?

• •

CHOOSING WHO IS first (or next) doesn't have to cause consternation. Try these strategies for classroom happiness.

For Small Group Play

■ Roll a die. Prior to rolling, the players decide if the highest or the lowest number goes first.

■ Draw a card from a numbered deck. Prior to drawing, the players decide if the highest or the lowest number goes first.

■ Cut several straws into different lengths. One player holds all of the straws in one hand so the lengths are unknown. Players draw straws. The length of each player's straw determines the sequence of play. Prior to drawing, the players decide if the longest or shortest straw goes first.

■ Play Rock, Paper, Scissors. Players simultaneously make a hand gesture to represent a rock (a fist), paper (flat hand), and scissors (two fingers extended). Rock breaks scissors, scissors cuts paper, and paper covers rock. This is typically done in pairs to determine a winner.

■ For two players or teams, one team flips a coin and the other team calls heads or tails. If the coin lands with the called side showing, the calling player/team is first. If the opposite side is showing, the flipping team is first.

■ Put marbles in a cloth bag using one for each player. All of the marbles are the same color except one. Each player selects a marble, without looking, and keeps it hidden in his or her hand. When all of the marbles have been chosen, the players open their hands. The player with the odd colored marble is first.

For Large Group Play

■ Have a container with each player's name in it. Names can be written on slips of paper or cards, milk caps, popsicle sticks, or tokens. Draw a name out of the container for first, second, and so on.

■ Play I'm Thinking of a Number. The game director tells the players a range of numbers and then thinks of a number in that range. The game director says, "I've got my number." Each player guesses a number. The player whose number is closest to the director's number goes first, next closest goes second, and so on.

■ Have a container of attributes such as brown eyes, black shoes, button shirt, a necklace, four letters in the first name, and so on written on slips of paper. Have all of the players standing. Draw and read an attribute. Players with that attribute can remain standing. Continue drawing and reading attributes until only one player is left standing.

■ Make a calendar for the month. On the last day of the month, students write their names on a day for the next month. If games are played on that day, the person whose name appears goes first or selects the player who is first. If you prefer, days could be divided in half to have more spaces.

■ Choose the first player by the one who is sitting most appropriately, has his or her desk cleared off, has all game supplies ready, and so on.

■ See who can be the fastest to find an item from inside his or her desk. Items might be an unsharpened pencil, a red crayon, a broken eraser, a bookmark with a cartoon character on it, or a library book with fewer than 30 pages.

Creating Teams

• •

As with picking who's first, choosing teams can be simple and fair. Try these methods.

■ Cut magazine pictures or drawings into pieces. Give each player a piece and the challenge to find the others with pieces from the same picture. (Tip: Mount the pictures on colored tagboard. Use various colors to designate the number of pieces to the puzzle. For example, use a red backing for teams of three, green for teams of four, and so on. Store the sets of pieces in a plastic bag.)

■ Use the game "Which One?" and freeze the game at any point during the questioning to create two teams from a larger group.

■ Decide the size of the team needed for the game or activity. Write the names of simple songs on cards that number of times. For example, if a team needs four players, write "Row, Row, Row Your Boat" on four cards; "Mary Had a Little Lamb" on another four cards; and so on. Players sing or hum the songs as they stroll around the room. Teams gather as they find others who are singing the same song.

■ Drawing short straws and long straws quickly separates a large group into two teams.

■ Small items that are readily sorted by color or another attribute can be pulled out of a cloth bag by each player. Players with items that match form a team.

Making Game Supplies and Pieces

• •

THE GAMES IN this book use some unusual pieces and boards, and this appendix provides suggestions for making pieces included in these game descriptions. It is written with a view to making these game pieces cost-conscious, durable, appealing, and easy to store. We encourage game mavens to keep an eye open at garage sales, thrift stores, and discount department stores for interesting items that can be used. Some of those items could even inspire a completely new game in themselves!

Game Boards

• •

The board for a game often sets the tone for the activity. Since boards will be used frequently, they need to be sturdy and yet easy to store. Interesting borders and pictures cut from magazines, printed from the computer, or hand drawn liven up empty spaces. Try writing in bubble letters or adding dots at the corners and intersecting lines of letters or adding extra loops to make any writing look more playful. Use watercolor markers or colored pencils for drawings and writing. (Permanent markers will occasionally bleed and crayons will melt when the game board is laminated or covered.) When the game board is complete, be sure to laminate thinner boards or use clear contact paper to protect stiff, thick boards that can't go through a laminating machine.

■ Tagboard or poster board, which comes in a multitude of colors, is a good weight for game boards and can be cut to any size. It can be purchased at variety, art, and office supply stores. Consider the size of your storage space when making an especially large game.

■ Recycle old game boards by mounting new ones over them. Fold or better yet cut the new game board in half before gluing to an old folding one. Test how the board closes before gluing permanently.

■ Change the look of a game by making a round game board. Using cardboard from a pizza is an easy way to get a sturdy, perfect circle. Pizzerias are sources for these.

■ Thin cardboard from pads of paper, weekly classroom magazines, and other packaging are free and frequently thrown away. This size stores easily in small plastic bags or folders.

■ Game boards can be drawn or mounted in standard and legal-sized folders. The front of the folder is a great place to write the directions for the game. Writing the game's name on the tab makes it easy to find when folded and stored in a file cabinet.

■ Gift boxes make great game boards, especially when it is advantageous for game pieces, dice, and so on, to be contained. Game boards can be cut to fit the box and either laid, glued, or hook and loop taped to the inside. Put all of the parts inside and the cover on and the game is all set to store. Write the game's name on the side and end of the cover so it is visible no matter how the box is stored.

■ Shower curtains can be made into large floor-sized game boards, as well as table-top games when cut into pieces. Permanent markers work well on these, and they come in appealing colors. These have the advantage of being easy to roll up and store when a flat board might take up too much space.

Game Pieces

The purpose or theme of a game can really be enhanced by selecting unique game pieces. Although standard tokens or pawns can be used, pieces specific to a game help make it more memorable and add a little extra fun.

Alternatively, keep a variety of game pieces in a container so players can make their own choices.

■ Cake decorations—Bakeries will often sell just the plastic pieces they use on top of specialty cakes.

■ Sets of plastic animals, space aliens, etc.—Dollar stores often carry this type of item.

■ Individually wrapped hard candy in different colors—As with anything, check to be sure that this follows any policies in place for your classroom, school, or district.

■ Buttons—Fabric stores often carry themed cards of four buttons such as flowers, vehicles, school symbols, and so on. Containers of assorted buttons can be found at rummage sales and antique shops.

■ Charms—Check the scrapbooking and jewelry-making sections of craft stores for these items.

■ Pom-poms—Students can individualize them by adding googly eyes and feet cut from tagboard.

■ Computer graphics—Select pictures using computer art or download from public domain sites. Using the computer, pictures can easily be sized for the game and printed. Gluing the pictures to tagboard, laminating, and cutting them out make them ready for use.

■ Party favors—Check party stores. If there isn't an assortment of colors, write or stick an identifying label on each piece. After playing a particular game a certain number of times, let the players keep their game pieces as a prize.

Dice

Dice are an integral part of many games. Commercially made dice are often available in red and green colors, so there is no need to use only white ones. Outlet or discount card shops often have dice in other colors or with different symbols on the sides with their holiday items.

■ Use foam for silent dice that don't disturb others. Cut foam into cubes with an electric knife or serrated knife. Foam can be purchased at fabric and upholstery shops. Cut foam to make extra large dice for games where a large group of players needs to see the same information.

■ Teacher supply stores and catalogs have dice that can be used on the overhead projector.

■ Teacher supply stores and catalogs have blank dice that can be written on. Use a permanent marker (can be erased with nail polish remover), adhesive dots, or a china marker to write on them.

■ Clear cubes sold for displaying photos make large, sturdy dice. Cut and design inserts for the cube's sides and slide the inserts in place. These inserts can be changed easily so cubes can be reused throughout the year.

■ Puzzle cubes make attractive, interesting dice. Each of the colored sides can indicate a particular consequence (be sure to include a key with the game) or adhesive labels can be placed on each side.

■ Use a pattern for paper cubes, as shown on the next page. This is a great way for players to create their own dice according to the needs of a game. Use construction paper or tagboard to make these more durable. After filling in each square, cut out the pattern and fold on each line. Complete the cube by gluing the tabs to the main portion of the die.

Cards

When designing cards for a game and determining how big to make them, consider the motor skills and size of your player's hands, the type or amount of information to be included on the cards, and the usual amount of space available for playing the game. Laminating the cards gives them a longer life.

■ Index cards come in various sizes and colors. They are quickly and easily cut into alternate sizes.

■ Save construction paper and tagboard pieces left over from other projects. When enough have been saved, use these scraps for cards.

■ Visit print shops, paper companies, and newspapers. Many times these businesses have cutoffs that they will give to teachers free for the asking.

■ If large sheets of tagboard are to be cut for cards, plan before cutting in order to use the whole sheet and to make the fewest cuts.

Paper Dice

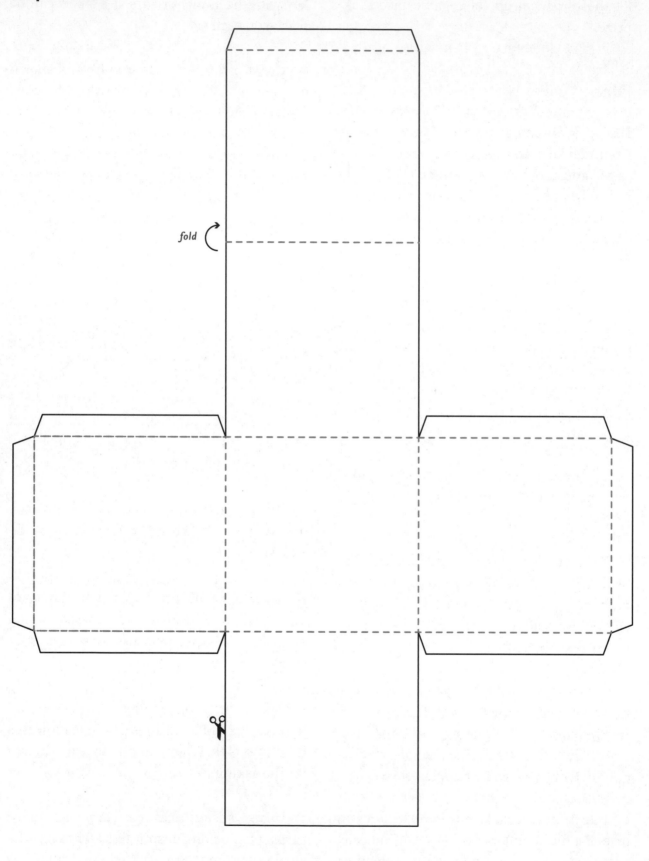

fold

Hook and Loop Tape

Hook and loop tape is a handy item available at variety, fabric, hardware, and even grocery stores. It comes in strips, dots, and squares. It is commonly found in black or white, but other colors such as navy and brown are also made. Make sure it has adhesive backing for easy application.

■ Use hook and loop tape to attach small plastic bags containing game parts/pieces to game boards.

■ Use hook and loop tape to attach answer sheets to the backs of game boards.

■ When using a folder with a flap opening for game storage, add a couple of pieces of hook and loop tape to the flap to keep it closed when not in use.

■ If a game has a board with cards or pieces that are moved, use hook and loop tape on the board and on the pieces. This quickly turns a floor or table game into one that can be hung on a wall or bulletin board.

■ Give recycled game boards a new top by using hook and loop tape in the corners of each.

Magnets

For matching or Concentration-style games, add a magnetic strip or dot to the cards so players can play the game on the marker board, side of a file cabinet, or other metal surface.

Response Sheets

Paper never seems to be in short supply in a classroom. Several of our games have sheets that can be copied or require blank paper. But there are alternatives as we try to conserve our resources. Plus there's an added benefit of using something other than paper. A change to something else makes the game automatically fun for the players!

■ Response boards are handy for players. These can be individual marker boards or chalkboards and even magic slates. Individual chalkboards can be made from scrap plywood or smooth paneling sprayed with chalkboard paint. Some chalkboard paints are even magnetic.

■ Ping-Pong paddles and folding fans work well for "yes/no," "true/false," or "higher/lower" type responses. Just write, tape, or use hook and loop tape to put the desired response on each side.

■ Make response sheets reusable by laminating them or placing them in sheet protectors or report covers. Crayons, china markers, dry-erase markers, and overhead markers work with varying results. Be sure to test these to determine which writes and erases the best on each surface before putting the game out to play.

■ Make copies of response sheets on transparencies. For these reusable sheets to function well for players, attach a plain piece of paper under the transparency with a paper clip and use overhead markers. There's an added benefit to creating response sheets this way.

They are great for game directors to use when demonstrating a new game or for players to share their answers with a larger group.

Laminating

To give a game more longevity and to avoid giving players unfair clues due to wear, laminate boards, cards, and any other flat pieces. If game boards or pieces have two layers, be sure the glue is thoroughly dry before laminating. Rubber cement keeps the layers smooth, but it often lets loose after a few months. To really solve this problem, dry-mount the layers to permanently bond them. (See the next section.) Prior to laminating cards and small pieces, cut them to size. Then when cutting them apart after laminating, leave a ⅛- to ¼-inch laminated margin around each piece. This helps keep the edges of pieces sealed to prevent peeling of the laminating film.

■ Use ends and scrap pieces of laminating film for players to write clues and words or to draw pictures on with overhead, permanent, or china markers. Use these on the overhead projector so everyone can see as well as hear.

■ Use scraps for clear pockets by cutting to size, placing them on the game board or chart, and taping around three sides. The clear pockets can hold different directions for the game, lists of new words or problems, and so on, to recycle or individualize the original game.

■ Larger ends of laminating film can be folded and taped along the sides to make clear folders to hold game boards and pieces.

Dry-Mount Tissue

Dry-mount tissue is a paper very similar in appearance to waxed paper. When dry-mount tissue is placed between two pieces of paper and heated, it will permanently adhere the two pieces of paper—unlike glue or rubber cement that often lets go as it ages. This is helpful because the game cards will still hold together if the laminated edges of the materials separate. Also, it allows you to cut the laminating film right to the edge of your cards or game pieces. You don't need to leave a margin. Using dry-mount tissue between two pieces of copy paper will make the paper stiff enough for game cards. Dry-mount tissue can be found in school, office, or photographic supply catalogs.

Keeping It All Together

It is frustrating to be excited about playing a game and then discover parts are missing. Efficient game storage is important to the players and in classroom management.

■ Use plastic containers to store game pieces by theme or game. They are also handy for game card storage. Wash and recycle various food containers for this. Don't forget baby food containers. They are especially handy for small game pieces and cards. Best of all, they stack well for storage.

■ Staple and then tape over the side edges of standard or legal-size file folders. Label the folder with the game's name. (Tip: Color-code the titles by subject area such as red for language arts, green for math, blue for science, and so on.) Directions for the game can be glued or written on the front of the folder. Store game pieces, cards, lists, and small game boards inside.

■ Plastic bags with sliding closures quickly store all game pieces and keep them visible. The 2-gallon size can even hold small game boards or sets of individual game boards. Use a permanent marker to label the bag with the name of the game. Punch a hole in a top corner of the bag and thread a large paper clip, shower curtain hook, or hinged ring through it. Now the bag can be displayed from a tack-strip or hung on a hook. Hang the bags on a hanger to store games when not in use.

■ Egg cartons can be used for storing game parts that need to be sorted. If more than 12 categories are needed, cut the base off of another egg carton of the same type. Cut its edge down about ¼ inch all the way around. This second section fits into the whole egg carton, which can still be closed for storage.

■ Artists' folders or portfolios can hold several game boards at once. Tagboard dividers can be put into the portfolio to group game boards by subject, level, or theme.

Grid Index

	M	Main Game
	V	Variation

L	Low
M	Moderate
H	High

TITLE	PG	Language Arts	Math	Science/Soc. Stud.	Strategy/Memory	Other	4	5	6	7	8	9	10	11	12	PLAYERS	NOISE LEVEL	ACTIVITY LEVEL
		— SUBJECT AREA					— AGE											
Back Words	22	M			M						•	•	•			6–10	M	M
Bake Me Some Pizza Pies	98		M							•	•	•	•			2–6	M	L
Basewordball	23	M									•	•	•	•		8–24	M–H	M–H
Bean Soup	100		M						•	•	•					2	L	L
Bed of Nails	206				M					•	•	•	•			3	M	M
Black Out	27	M			M					•	•	•	•	•		2–24	L–M	L
Bolt to the End	2	M	M	M	M							•	•	•	•	5–13	M–H	M
Box Top Tops	28	M	V							•	•	•	•	•		2–6	M	L
Bracelet Race	102		M						•	•	•					2–5	M	L
Bug Bite	32	M	V						•	•	•	•				2–4	M–H	L–M
Bull's-Eye Feather Math	107		M								•	•	•	•	•	2–4	M	L
Buttons in a Box	111		M								•	•	•			4	M	L–M

235

			Main Game										L	Low					
M	Main Game												M	Moderate					
V	Variation												H	High					

TITLE	PG	Language Arts	Math	Science/Soc. Stud.	Strategy/Memory	Other	4	5	6	7	8	9	10	11	12	PLAYERS	NOISE LEVEL	ACTIVITY LEVEL
		SUBJECT AREA					AGE											
Character Guess	33	M			V	M			•	•	•	•	•	•	•	2–8	L	L
Clock Race	112		M						•	•	•	•	•			2–4	L	L
Common Threads	4	M	M	M		M	•	•	•	•	•	•	•	•	•	3–8	M–H	L
Concentrate on the Meaning	36	M	V	V	M						•	•	•	•		2	L	L
Connect-O	113	V	M					•	•							2–12	L–M	L
Crazy Cuts	114		M		M						•	•	•	•		2–8	M	M
Cross Out	38	M			M	M					•	•	•	•	•	2–8	L	L
Dice-O	115		M		M							•	•	•		2–6	L–M	L
Dipping and Dripping Rhymes	39	M									•	•	•	•		2–6	M	M
Don't Say "It"	41	M		M								•	•	•	•	2–6	M–H	M
Down the Hall and Up the Elevator	117		M	V	M							•	•	•		2–4	L	L
Egg Money	119		M		M				•	•	•					2–3	M	L
Egg-straordinary Words	45	M										•	•	•	•	2–6	M	L
Egg-streme Matching	180	M		M									•	•	•	2–4	M	L
50 or Bust!	122		M									•	•	•	•	2–24	L	L
Fishy Facts	6	M	M	M					•	•	•					2–4	M	L
Flower Garden	46	M	V	V					•	•	•					2–4	M	L
Flying Feather Race	185			M							•	•	•	•	•	2–4	M	M
Fractured Proverbs	48	M			V	M					•	•	•			2	M	L

Grid Index

Grid Index

M Main Game **V** Variation

L Low **M** Moderate **H** High

		SUBJECT AREA					AGE											
TITLE	PG	Language Arts	Math	Science/Soc. Stud.	Strategy/Memory	Other	4	5	6	7	8	9	10	11	12	PLAYERS	NOISE LEVEL	ACTIVITY LEVEL
Quintessential Game	70	M		M		M						•	•	•	•	3–10	M	L
Rainbow	73	M				M	•	•	•							2–4	L	L
Red Word, Green Word	76	M	V							•	•	•	•	•		2–4	L–M	L
Rubber-Band Rodeo	15	M	M	M					•	•	•	•	•			2	L	L
The Ruler Rules	154		M								•	•	•	•		4–24	M–H	H
Scratch My Back	77	M							•	•	•	•				3–5	M	L
Secret Message	156	M	M			M			•	•	•					2–10	L	L
Sentence Please	80	M										•	•	•	•	2–6	L	L
Shoebox	81	M										•	•			2–6	M	L
Shop 'Til You Drop	86	M								•	•	•				4–6	M	L
Speed Limit	158		M									•	•	•	•	2–6	M	L
Sum Big Fish	162		M								•	•	•	•		2–6	L	L
Sum of the String	165		M									•	•	•	•	2–4	M	L
Sum Thinking	168		M		M							•	•	•	•	2–6	L	L
Superlative Scavenger Hunt	87	M									•	•	•	•	•	6–24	M	H
Switcho Change–O	89	M										•	•	•	•	2–8	M	L
Taking a Trip	217	M	M	M	M							•	•	•	•	4–20	M	L–M
Taking Tokens	171		M									•	•	•	•	6	L–M	L
Team Towers	199			M	M			•	•	•	•	•	•	•	•	5–11	M	M

Legend:
- M — Main Game
- V — Variation
- L — Low
- M — Moderate
- H — High

Grid Index

Skills Index

Beginning Skills

Colors

Ice Cream Colors, 56
Rainbow, 73

Letters

Identification
Hopscotch Challenge, 50

Phonetic Awareness
Box Top Tops—variation, 28
Flower Garden, 46
Scratch My Back—variation, 77
Shop 'Til You Drop, 86
Taking a Trip, 217

Sequence
Connect-O—variation, 113
Get in Line, 7
Hopscotch Challenge, 50

Uppercase/Lowercase
Egg-streme Matching—variation, 180
Flower Garden—variation, 46

Numbers

Identification
Flower Garden—variation, 46
Hopscotch Challenge—variation, 50
Secret Message, 156
What's My Name?, 220

Sequence
Connect-O, 113
Get in Line, 7
Hopscotch Challenge—variation, 50

Patterning

Bracelet Race, 102

Shape Identification

Polygon Crossing, 149

Visual Discrimination

Hide and Seeds, 8

General Knowledge Skills

◼ Art

Progressive Pictures, 68

◼ Categorizing

Junk Drawer, 211

◼ Music

Humdinger, 54
Progressive Pictures—variation, 68

◼ Proverbs

Fractured Proverbs, 48

◼ Record Keeping

Hide and Seeds, 8
Which One?—variation, 17

◼ Venn Diagram

Junk Drawer—variation, 211

Language Arts Skills

◼ Creative Writing

Let's Go Shopping—variation, 132
Pass a Laugh, 63
Progressive Pictures—variation, 68
Sentence Please, 80
Switcho Change-O, 89
Who, What, When, Where, Why, and
     How?, 92

◼ Reading

Characterization
Character Guess, 33

Comprehension
Black Out, 27
Character Guess, 33
Fractured Proverbs, 48
Odd One Wins!, The, 61

Phonics
Shop 'Til You Drop, 86

Retelling,
Humdinger—variation, 54

Story Elements
Picture This, 64
Who, What, When, Where, Why, and
     How?—variation, 92

Words
Back Words, 22
Black Out, 27
Bug Bite, 32
Dipping and Dripping Rhymes, 39
Geographic Name Chain, 188
Got the Time?, 125
Hide and Seeds, 8
On the Hunt, 62
Popular Picks, 67
Red Word, Green Word, 76
Secret Message, 156
Shoebox, 81

◼ Speaking

Don't Say "It", 41
Humdinger, 54
Picture This, 64

Science Skills

■ Content

Social Studies Skills

■ Content

■ Map Skills

Atlas and Map Reading

Coordinates

States and Capitals

Thinking Skills

■ Logic

■ Memory

About the Authors

ALEXIS LUDEWIG has been an educator since 1970. She has experience as an elementary classroom, Title I/Chapter 1 Language Arts and Math, and Resource Teacher. In 2002, she was selected as the Wisconsin Teacher of the Year. Her classroom is a lively blend of various learning environments and technology. Alexis serves on the Teacher Advisory Council and the Blue Ribbon Technology Council for REL Midwest (Regional Education Laboratory) and Learning Point. She was the recipient of a Scholastic, Inc. Fellowship, which sent her to Scholastic's headquarters in New York City to work in the development of the Scholastic RED program (a professional educators' online program emphasizing best practices in reading) and their professional books division. She has since reviewed/edited books for Scholastic, Inc., McGraw-Hill, Inc., and Corwin Press.

DR. AMY SWAN completed her graduate studies in Educational Psychology and School Psychology at the University of Michigan after becoming certified as an elementary teacher. Her 19 years of professional experience have been in public and private schools in the United States as well as the Caribbean, working with students from preschool through college age as an educator, diagnostician, supervisor, and counselor. As a parent, she enjoys party planning for children and adults with an emphasis on themed activities and games that span the ages.

MORE HELPFUL RESOURCES FOR YOUR CLASSROOM

The Organized Teacher
Springer, Alexander, and Persiani-Becker

Perfect for first-year teachers of grades K–8, *The Organized Teacher* covers everything from classroom management and school procedures to streamlined record keeping and state standards.

$19.95

The Creative Teacher
Springer, Alexander, and Persiani-Becker

Discover hundreds of creative ideas to reenergize your lesson plans for any subject, across all grades—from waking up the tired book report to making math fun.

$19.95

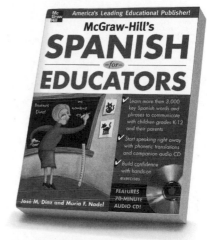

McGraw-Hill's Spanish for Educators
Díaz and Nadel

This book and audio CD course offers you more than 3,000 essential Spanish words and phrases and the basic grammar needed to use them properly and with confidence.

$19.95

The Teacher's Calendar
The Editors of Chase's

The Teacher's Calendar offers you innovative classroom ideas for every day of the year, from August 1 to July 31. Each page is packed with suggestions for classroom activities, bulletin boards, and school calendars.

$19.95

Teach Terrific Writing, Grades 4–5
&
Teach Terrific Writing, Grades 6–8
Muschla

Help your students clarify their thoughts, put them down on paper, and proofread and revise their own work with these unique resources. Each book includes reproducible worksheets and activities, answer keys, and "Teachers' Notes."

$19.95 each

Teach Terrific Grammar, Grades 4–5
&
Teach Terrific Grammar, Grades 6–8
Muschla

With more than 170 reproducible grammar activities and puzzles, these indispensable guides contain everything a language arts or substitute teacher needs to present grammar topics.

$19.95 each

Learn more. Do more.
MHPROFESSIONAL.COM

These and other great books from the McGraw-Hill Teacher Resource library are available at your favorite local or online book retailer.